ISSUES IN POLITICAL THEORY

Political Theory has undergone a remarkable development in recent years. From a state in which it was once declared dead, it has come to occupy a central place in the study of Politics. Both political ideas and the wide-ranging arguments to which they give rise are now treated in a rigorous, analytical fashion, and political theorists have contributed to disciplines as diverse as economics, sociology and law. These developments have made the subject more challenging and exciting, but they have also added to the difficulties of students and others coming to the subject for the first time. Much of the burgeoning literature in specialist books and journals is readily intelligible only to those who are already well-versed in the subject.

Issues in Political Theory is a series conceived in response to this situation. It consists of a number of detailed and comprehensive studies of issues central to Political Theory which take account of the latest developments in scholarly debate. While making original contributions to the subject, books in the series are written especially for those who are new to Political Theory. Each volume aims to introduce its readers to the intricacies of a fundamental political issue and to help them find their way through the detailed, and often complicated, argument that this issue has attracted.

PETER JONES
ALBERT WEALE

ISSUES IN POLITICAL THEORY

Series editors: PETER JONES and ALBERT WEALE

Published

Christopher J. Berry: **Human Nature**
Michael Lessnoff: **Social Contract**
Richard Lindley: **Autonomy**
Andrew Reeve: **Property**

Forthcoming

David Beetham: **Legitimacy**
Tom Campbell: **Justice**
Tim Gray: **Freedom**
John Horton: **Political Obligation**
Peter Jones: **Rights**
Susan Mendus: **Toleration and the Limits of Liberty**
Raymond Plant: **Equality**
Hillel Steiner: **Utilitarianism**

Autonomy

Richard Lindley

Humanities Press International, Inc.
Atlantic Highlands, NJ

First published in 1986 in the United States of America by
HUMANITIES PRESS INTERNATIONAL, INC.,
Atlantic Highlands, NJ 07716

Library of Congress Cataloging-in-Publication Data
Lindley, Richard.
  Autonomy.
  (Issues in political theory)
  Bibliography: p.
  Includes index.
  1. Liberty. 2. Democracy. 3. Autonomy. I. Title.
II. Series.
JC571.L555   1986   323.44   86–2913
ISBN 0–391–03429–4
ISBN 0–391–03428–6 (pbk.)

PRINTED IN HONG KONG

For Emma, Joe, Lenny, Sam and Tam

Contents

Acknowledgements   x

1 **Introduction**   **1**
   Concepts and conceptions   2
   Autonomy – the basic concept   5
   Liberal democracy   7

PART I CONCEPTIONS   **11**

2 **Autonomy as Pure Rationality**   **13**
   Rationality and autonomy   14
   The Kantian view   16
   Pure rationality   17
   The worth of people   20
   Rationality and authorship   21
   Autonomy, freedom and responsibility   22
   Reasons and emotions   26
   Conclusion   27

3 **The Destruction of the Whole World**   **28**
   The ultimate ends of human action   29
   Autonomy and freedom   32
   Deliberation   33
   Neutrality   37
   Irrational desires   39
   Desires, reasons and action   41
   Conclusion   42

4 **Socrates and the Fool**   **44**
   Brave New World   44
   Theoretical rationality   46

Truth	48
Self-determination and self-realisation	52
Mill's theory considered	55
Conclusion	61

5 A Liberal Conception of Autonomy — **63**
Conative heteronomy	63
Freedom of the will and levels of desire	64
Weakness of will	67
Being autonomous and exercising autonomy	68
The conception	69
Conclusion	70

PART II PRINCIPLES — **71**

6 Respect for Autonomy — **73**
Different attitudes towards values	73
Conflicts	74
Neutrality and the goal of autonomy	82
Now, rationality and morality	91
Conclusion	93

7 The Liberty Principle — **95**
Moral theory, political theory and political science	96
The state and individual liberty	102
The general problem	109
Conclusion	112

PART III PRACTICES — **115**

8 Children — **117**
The received view	118
Respect for children	120
Are children people?	121
The vote	125
Education	133
Conclusion	139

9 Mental Disorder — **140**
Mental handicap	140
Mental illness	145

Illness 145
Treatment 150
Taking seriously the autonomy of mental patients 158
Conclusion 163

10 False Consciousness and Emancipation 165
False consciousness 166
The paradox of emancipation 168
Real interests 170
Autonomy, interests and perfectionism 177
Conclusion 184

11 Concluding Remarks 186

Guide to Further Reading 190

Bibliography 192

Index 196

Acknowledgements

I am grateful to many people who have helped me, in various ways, to write this book. I would first like to thank Peter Jones and Albert Weale, not only for asking me to write the book, but also for being such helpful and enthusiastic editors.

Over the last ten years my colleagues at Bradford, especially Roger Fellows and Graham Macdonald, have provided me with support, encouragement, and many excellent discussions.

I have learnt a lot from conversations with Gregory DesJardins, Jonathan Glover, John Harris, Jim Hopkins, Philip Pettit, Mel Sayers, Pete Sayers and Tom Sorell.

Keith Graham, Jeremy Holmes, Peter Jones, Anthony O'Hear, Derek Parfit, and Albert Weale all gave me written comments on an earlier draft, which have spared me many embarrassments and greatly improved the book.

I am most grateful to John M. Baker who generously wrote extensive, very detailed comments on my first draft. His incisive criticisms led me to see clearly a number of serious difficulties with my ideas, and his constructive suggestions helped me to try to sort them out.

I would like to thank my parents for their continuing encouragement, and for helping me to acquire a word-processor.

I owe most to my co-parent Errollyn Bruce. Although no lover of philosophy, she has always been prepared to discuss ideas for the book with me. I gathered many of the more worthwhile ideas for the book from her. Without her unfailing friendship this book would not have been written.

Finally, I would like to thank Richard Hall, for his conscientious proof-reading. Any remaining errors are my responsibility.

Richard Lindley

1 Introduction

What is autonomy? Why is it valuable? How important is autonomy compared to other values? How should autonomy be promoted in society? Is autonomy properly respected? These are some of the questions which I hope to tackle in this book. The task is difficult because none of these questions seems to have a clear-cut answer. There has been, and probably will continue to be, much controversy over all of them. Does it matter that there are such disputes, in particular, about the *meaning* of 'autonomy', and to what extent can they be resolved?

'If ants were called elephants, and elephants were called ants, I'd be able to squash an elephant'. So goes a song by Danny Kaye. It really doesn't matter whether we use the word 'elephant' to refer to elephants, or choose some other word, such as 'ant' – as long as we are clear which. Changing the meanings of the words 'elephant' and 'ant' wouldn't materially affect our capacities, or our beliefs about the desirability of staying out of the path of oncoming elephants, and protecting our larders from invasion by ants.

In contrast, the meanings which are given to key concepts in politics can have great significance. Consider the following example: On 17 September 1978 an historic agreement was signed by President Jimmy Carter of the United States, President Anwar Sadat of Egypt, and Prime Minister Menachim Begin of Israel. It would end the state of war between Egypt and Israel, and supposedly offered a solution to the Palestinian problem, which has been at the heart of the Middle East conflict since 1948. Sinai was returned to Egypt by Israel, and the Israelis agreed to offer 'autonomy' to the Palestinian Arabs living in the West Bank and Gaza regions. It was no coincidence that the agreement did not define 'autonomy'. Autonomy is, whatever it is, something apparently to be treasured; so the Israelis hoped they would be

1

seen as having conceded something of value, and the Egyptians hoped they would be seen as having won something significant for the Palestinians.

It has since emerged that what the Israelis understood by 'autonomy' in the context of the Camp David Agreement is a very limited form of administrative control over some day-to-day affairs. If the Israelis have their way the lands over which the Palestinians might have 'autonomy' would come permanently under Israeli sovereignty, and the Israelis would maintain complete control over such vital matters as internal security and foreign policy. On the other hand the Egyptians understand by 'autonomy' something far more substantial. For them 'autonomy' means no less than 'self-government', perhaps in the sense of territorial sovereignty. Which interpretation is correct? What is the method for finding out?

In one sense there is no correct answer to such a dispute about the meaning of the word 'autonomy'. The view that there is a Platonic Form of Autonomy – the true, eternal definition, waiting to be uncovered by philosophers, is hard to sustain, and will not be defended here.

Definitions are usually records of the conventions of particular social groups. With controversial concepts such as 'autonomy' one may expect to find different, though related ideas being considered under the umbrella of the key word. 'Democracy' is the description favoured by politicians in Britain and North America, to describe the political systems which operate there. Equally it is built into the very *name* of the Deutsche Demokratische Republik of East Germany, where a radically different system operates.

Concepts and conceptions

The East German and United States governments may disagree about which of their respective political systems is democratic, whereas others may claim that neither is truly democratic. However, in order for any of them to *disagree* it is necessary that they *agree* on something. Otherwise, at most their disagreement would be purely terminological, of the sort one could imagine having with someone who thought that the word 'elephant' referred to ants, and went on to claim that it was easy to squash elephants. The disagreement would not be substantive, because the two parties would be talking about different things. The disputants about democracy are talking about the same thing; but they disagree about its nature. In so far as there is argument over the meaning of 'democracy' the disputants *agree* about the basic concept, but disagree about how the concept is to be interpreted. Similarly with autonomy: disputants may disagree about how 'autonomy' is to be analysed, but they do share the same basic concept.

One way of bringing this out is to draw a distinction between *concepts* and *conceptions* of those concepts (see Rawls, 1971, Chapter 1). The Egyptian and Israeli negotiators at Camp David used the same concept, 'autonomy', in their agreement, even though they may have different conceptions of that concept. A conception is a particular interpretation or analysis of a concept. Although there is no eternally true conception of autonomy, the concept being a tool invented by human beings to make distinctions thought to be useful, it may be possible to test rival conceptions for *adequacy*. There are better and worse conceptions – at least relative to different values.

An adequate conception must fall within the scope of the basic concept. Any conception of autonomy which entailed that people are autonomous if and only if they are never able to make any decisions about how to live their lives, would clearly be inadequate to the concept.

One reason for the disputes over rival conceptions of many political concepts is that these concepts are used with powerful evaluative force. Thus, 'democracy', 'freedom' and 'peace' are all thought to be so valuable to a decent life, that the claim, say, that a policy is essential for the protection of democracy immediately lends that policy support. Autonomy is, certainly within liberal democratic societies, such a concept. The autonomy of the individual is held to be vitally important. Therefore any adequate *liberal* conception of autonomy must be consistent with autonomy having this status. An adequate conception will, ideally, be an interpretation of 'autonomy' which will make it clear why autonomy is held in such high regard. Of course this does not entail that the conception has to show that autonomy really is desirable, but only to render explicable why it is thought to be. This part of a justification of a conception is likely to be controversial, since there are disagreements about what constitutes a desirable political system or way of life. This task does not, as some may think, require the positing and defence of a set of values which are objectively correct in the sense that they would have to be accepted by *any* rational, correctly informed person, from any historical circumstances. In order for there to be any point in defending a particular conception, one has simply to assume that there is some agreement, at least amongst parties to the discussion, over fundamental values. Conceptions are adequate relative to different sets of values. Thus, although one might be unable to persuade a liberal democrat, a Nazi and a Moonie to agree upon a conception of autonomy, there should be a true 'liberal' conception – that is, one which is adequate to the concept, as interpreted in the light of liberal values.

Any attempt to persuade someone to change his values will, if successful, have to appeal to some common values in order to carry any weight. The normative arguments in this book are primarily addressed to those who are impressed by the attractions of liberal democracy.

Another task for a political theorist investigating autonomy is to discuss the commitments implied by taking seriously one or other conception of autonomy. One is particularly interested in the commitments implicit in taking autonomy seriously, as interpreted by an adequate conception. The prime reason for presenting political arguments is to persuade people. The desired method of political philosophy is to attempt to persuade people by rational argument. Such arguments do not, however, need to use only premises which no rational being could question. Many arguments will be of the form: 'If you accept *A*, then you should accept *B*. You do accept *A*. Therefore you should accept *B*.' Such arguments may not be expected to carry much practical significance for those who do not accept *A*. However, if one correctly identifies a dominant value in society, one has a powerful critical tool. Suppose we can agree that people's autonomy should be respected, and we can agree on a conception of autonomy. It is now possible to describe the sorts of policies which are consistent with taking seriously the principle that autonomy should be respected. One may then be in a position to argue that the society in question fails (and perhaps cannot but fail) to take seriously its own values.

In the final part of this book I shall look at the implications of taking seriously a commitment to the value of autonomy – in three cases where people's capacity for autonomy may be thought to be deficient. I shall compare present attitudes and policies towards children and the mentally disordered with what would be required by showing respect for their autonomy. I shall then discuss the thorny problem of false consciousness – which concerns the possible loss of autonomy amongst 'normal' people who are perhaps unaware of their own real interests. How should one regard the present (perhaps non-autonomous) preferences of people whose autonomy has been impaired by poor socialisation and/or the generation of crucial false assumptions about the nature of society? My first task, however, is to describe the basic concept of autonomy.

Autonomy – the basic concept

The example I gave about a dispute over the meaning of 'autonomy' – the Camp David Agreement – concerned regional autonomy. It was a question about the extent to which the Palestinians should control the territory in which they lived. 'Autonomy' has its etymological roots in the two Greek words for 'self', and 'rule' or 'law'. Thus autonomy is literally 'self-rule'. We may speak of social groups, such as nations, government departments, committees, and professional associations being autonomous, being in control of their own affairs, or more tendentiously, being a law unto themselves. People may object to a committee being too autonomous. What is usually being expressed here is the belief that the committee should be more *accountable* to the community, or to those who are affected by its deliberations. It snould be more representative. Although autonomy is not always thought desirable for committees or representative bodies, we accept that national groups seek autonomy, and the principle of nation states having the right to rule themselves is at least theoretically enshrined in international conventions. As the example of the Camp David Agreement shows there is considerable controversy about what 'self-rule' means in the context of territories and national groups. Although there are many important questions concerning regional autonomy, the main theme of this book is not 'group autonomy', but a concept which has been central to the liberal tradition, certainly since before the heyday of nineteenth-century imperialism. I mean 'individual autonomy'. This is the self-rule of the individual in society. It has been regarded as of enormous importance in the Western political tradition, certainly since the late eighteenth century. But what *is* the basic concept of individual autonomy? I think the underlying idea of the concept of autonomy is self-mastery. This means both mastery over one's self, and one's self not being subservient to others. It is well expressed in Isaiah Berlin's characterisation of people's wish for what he calls 'positive liberty':

'I wish my life and decisions to depend on myself, not on external forces of whatever kind. I wish to be the instrument of my own, not of other men's, acts of will. I wish to be a subject, not an object; to be moved by reasons, by conscious purposes, which are my own, not by causes which affect me, as it were, from outside. I wish to be somebody, not nobody; a doer – deciding, not being decided for, self-directed and not acted on by external nature or by other men as if I were a thing, or an animal, or a slave incapable of playing a human role, that is, of conceiving goals and policies of my own and realizing them . . . I wish, above all, to be conscious of myself as a thinking, willing, active being, bearing responsibility for my choices and able to explain them by references to my own ideas and purposes.' (Berlin, 1958, p.131)

The two dimensions of autonomy are well brought out in this statement. To be autonomous requires, first of all, that one have a developed self, to which one's actions can be ascribed. This in turn requires a consciousness of oneself as a being who acts for reasons, whose behaviour can be explained by reference to one's own goals and purposes.

The other dimension of autonomy requires a freedom from external constraints. An autonomous person is not someone who is manipulated by others, or who is forced to do their will. An autonomous person has a will of her or his own, and is able to act in pursuit of self-chosen goals. I shall not offer an account of the self, which could easily fill a book on its own. I hope that what I do say about the self will, on the whole, be uncontentious.

Most of the first half of the book will be a comparison of three influential and, I think, intrinsically interesting, conceptions of autonomy. There are many conceptions of autonomy. I could, for example, have profitably discussed Buddhist, Stoic, psychoanalytic, or existentialist conceptions.

In selecting the three conceptions that I have for discussion, I have taken account of the fact that this is a book in a series on issues in political theory. I have also borne in mind that 'autonomy' is a value which lies near the heart of the prevailing official systems of values in what I shall call 'liberal democratic' societies, from which most of the readers of this book will come.

The conceptions of autonomy which I shall discuss have been significant in shaping liberal democratic thought about the state and the individual. By narrowing the focus of discussion I hope better to be able to cast a critical eye on liberal democracy, using as a yardstick its own professed values, particularly the quintessential value of individual autonomy.

Liberal democracy

At various places in this book, especially in the second half, I shall refer to 'liberal democracy' as a generic term for the sort of political system which the United States, United Kingdom, the countries of Western Europe, Canada, Australia and New Zealand, to name some, have in common. There are no doubt important differences, especially in the dominant political institutions in these countries. However, they do share a set of salient properties which makes it useful to group them together as 'liberal democracies'. What are these properties?

First, they are all pluralist, multi-party representative democracies. Governments are elected for limited terms, by a universal franchise of adults. Elections are contests between rival political parties, who compete for the popular vote, on the strength, among other things, of different policies.

Second, they all allow, and officially celebrate, freedom of speech, freedom of the press, freedom of thought and freedom of conscience. Freedom of expression is held to be vitally important, and it is regarded as a fundamental citizen's right to express opinions which may be critical of the government in power. Such freedoms are often spoken of as 'negative' liberties, being freedoms from governmental restrictions. It is essential to liberal democracy that there be a large area of personal life where the individual is not subject to governmental interference (see Berlin, 1958, for an account of the distinction between positive and negative liberty).

Finally, the mode of production in liberal democracies is predominantly capitalist. In all of these countries, to a greater or lesser extent, the state intervenes in the market place – notably in health, education and welfare; and some industries are nationalised. However, the chief determinant of production is making profits in the market, and the means of production are predominantly privately owned.

In his interesting study, C. B. Macpherson (1977) argued that there is a deep tension within liberal democracy between its commitment to a predominantly capitalist economic system, and its insistence on 'the claim of equal individual rights to self-development' (p.1). I agree with Macpherson that a recognition of the importance of these rights is at the heart of the justification for liberal democracy. Why are liberal democracies thought to be better than the Soviet Union and its satellites? Because they apparently better promote people's equal individual rights to self-development.

Isaiah Berlin distinguishes, as we have seen, two concepts of liberty – the former, negative liberty, to do with the area of non-interference by society in the life of the individual, the second, positive liberty, or autonomy, to do with who or what controls an individual's life.

Berlin offers a strong warning against political leaders and writers who seek to 'liberate' people – in the sense of granting them their positive liberty. True liberalism seeks to defend people's negative liberties, and leaves their positive liberty well alone.

Whilst accepting that calls for greater positive liberty may appear to legitimise far-reaching coercion of people in the name of their own 'liberation', I believe that the main rationale for favouring a large sphere of negative liberty is that it may be essential for the promotion of autonomy, which is a more fundamental value. If people were incapable of controlling their own lives, or were such self-determination unimportant, it would matter far less if the sphere of influence of the state were greatly extended.

Similarly, if there were no value in people shaping their own destiny, it would be a matter of little concern whether or not a country was democratic or run by a benevolent dictator. And yet benevolent dictatorship is widely, and I think rightly, thought to be abhorrent. One way round the problem of the potential abuse of the concept of autonomy is to offer an adequate liberal conception.

Liberal democracy is premised on the assumption that people should have equal rights to run their own lives. This in turn depends on a view of people as the proper objects of respect. The claim made by Macpherson is that, far from promoting people's equal individual rights to self-development, capitalist societies actually deny such rights to many. This charge will be considered in Part III of the book.

It is clear that morally the claim that people should have equal rights to run their own lives carries more weight than the claim that society should be run on capitalist economic principles. It would be bizarre if a liberal democrat sought to defend the present organisation of society on the grounds that, although it did not properly protect people's rights to run their own lives, at least it is capitalist. Indeed, the values of liberal democracy, which lead to the belief in civil and political liberties, are not *essentially* tied to a particular economic system. Among 'liberal democrats', as I am using the expression, we may include some conservatives, nearly all social democrats, and most who would call themselves socialists.

A political scientist would probably begin a study of liberal democracies by offering a detailed analysis of the political institutions of such societies, showing how various forms of political organisation produce, perhaps inexorably, certain consequences. Although there would inevitably be some implicit or explicit discussion of values, these would be secondary to the political analysis. With political theory or political philosophy (I use these terms interchangeably) the emphasis is the other way round. The prime focus is the values of such societies. There may be some discussion of how the values work out in practice; but a *detailed study* is beyond the scope of political theory as such.

So the prime aim of this book is to elucidate liberal conceptions of autonomy, with a view to gaining a clearer insight into the strengths and weaknesses of liberal democracies, from the perspective of their own official values.

PART I

CONCEPTIONS

In this part of the book there will be a discussion of three rival conceptions of autonomy from within the liberal tradition. The conceptions derive from Immanuel Kant (1724–1804), David Hume (1711–76), and John Stuart Mill (1806–73). I have chosen these conceptions because each is both philosophically interesting, and of great importance to the liberal tradition.

Although I start by considering views associated with historical figures, this is not a work in the history of ideas. I realise that fully to do justice to the political ideas of the above thinkers would require at least a book for each of them. I call the conceptions to be discussed 'Kantian', 'Humean' and 'Millian', to imply that although their ancestry may be traced back to the three great philosophers, they are not necessarily conceptions which the three would fully endorse. I could have given the conceptions non-personalised labels, but I think this would have been a worse insult to Kant, Hume and Mill than the rather brief treatment given their writings below.

My main concern in this part is to characterise and test for adequacy the three conceptions. Discussion of the application of principles of respect for autonomy will be reserved for later in the book.

2 Autonomy as Pure Rationality

'Act in such a way that you always treat humanity, whether in your own person or in the person of any other, never simply as a means, but always at the same time as an end.' (Kant, 1785)

For thousands of years human beings have farmed. We grow crops and rear animals for food. Recently these practices have been criticised from a variety of angles: we have damaged soil through over-use; our use of the land is very wasteful; many starve, whilst others live a life of excessive luxury; our treatment of animals in modern factory farms is cruel . . . the list is endless. However nobody, as far as I know, thinks that there is anything wrong in principle with growing crops simply to feed ourselves, and most people think it is all right to rear animals for food, provided that they are not made to suffer.

Imagine now a society where 'humane' human farming was practised. The society is governed by a cannibalistic aristocracy of scientists. They have developed sophisticated techniques of brain control, so that they are able to produce a population of compliant slaves. Throughout their lives, during which they are well-fed, and offered many amusements, the slaves' main pleasure comes from serving their masters, and indeed they have very pleasureful lives. When the time comes for them to be killed for the table, they experience little fear, and are glad that the main purpose of their life is soon to be realised. All this is achieved through the Ministry of Harmony, whose function is so to programme the slave class that they will serve the ends of the masters with minimum conflict.

This would be a society of far less suffering than our own, and yet. . . . And yet the dream is not a utopian vision of an ideal society, but a nightmare. Although the 'farming' methods of this community are far less cruel in many ways than our own practices of animal husbandry, something is drastically wrong in this imagined world. What?

Perhaps the best way to express what is wrong is to say that this is a society where no respect is shown for people's autonomy. Happily the only context in which the policies of such a society are likely to be proposed is in a satirical work of fiction such as Jonathan Swift's classic work on the Irish Problem. This is because it is widely accepted that autonomy is an essential characteristic of humanity, and that it is wrong to treat autonomous beings simply as means to ends. We exist as ends in ourselves.

Certainly for the last 150 years (with a few breaks) the view that people should be treated as ends has been very widely recognised in liberal democracies. In what sense is it true that people are, and should be treated as 'ends in themselves'? What are ends in themselves?

Rationality and autonomy

The philosopher most closely associated with the view that human beings, in virtue of our autonomy, should treat each other as ends in ourselves, is Immanuel Kant. I shall therefore begin with discussion of a Kantian conception of autonomy.

Plants and lower animals are not autonomous because they lack rationality; on the other hand people are autonomous – apparently because we possess rationality. What is the connection between rationality and autonomy? This difficult question is complicated by the fact that there are two concepts of rationality.

The chief function of the first is to divide creatures into those with certain intellectual capacities, and the rest. A rational creature is one who is able to reason; and act through arriving at beliefs and desires, the product of such reasoning. People are rational, whereas prawns, trees and stones are non-rational, since they all lack the requisite intellectual abilities. They are unable to act in pursuit of goals which they have set themselves in the light of deliberation. All creatures are either rational or non-rational.

I shall call this kind of rationality 'possessing a will'. To have a will to do something is to have resolved to do it, even though the action may be contrary to present inclination. This requires the capacity to reflect, to form a view of the world which is not simply that given by present appearance or attraction. All and only creatures with a will can act for reasons. The behaviour of a creature which acts for reasons can best be explained by citing its reasons, rather than, for instance, by citing physical laws. There is a sense in which such creatures are 'a law unto themselves' – with their own purposes and view of the world. We could, therefore, call all creatures with a will 'autonomous'. So all creatures are either autonomous or non-autonomous, and the non-autonomous are none other than the non-rational. In future I shall use the description 'possessing a will' to refer to all creatures which are not non-rational and (the same group) all creatures which are not non-autonomous.

In addition to the distinction between creatures with a will and the rest, we use other concepts when we speak of a person being particularly rational, or especially autonomous. Here the opposite of 'rational' is not 'non-rational' but 'irrational'; the opposite of 'autonomous' is not 'non-autonomous', but 'heteronomous'.

If a prawn swims into a shrimping net this is disastrous for the prawn; but it is not irrational, because prawns do not have wills. A prawn is unable to act deliberatively. The charge 'irrational' is the most general form of criticism which can be levelled against creatures with a will. Its primary targets are beliefs, desires, emotions and actions, which fail to meet ideal standards of deliberation and execution. I include the latter, because one form of irrationality is to act against one's better judgment, even against the conclusions of unimpaired deliberation. In what follows I shall, barring specific, stated exceptions, mean by 'rational' the opposite of 'irrational', rather than 'possessing a will', and by 'autonomous' the opposite of 'heteronomous' (I deliberately talk of autonomous and rational *creatures*, so as not to define out of existence the possibility of non-human beings with a will). The unfortunate prawn is no more heteronomous than it is irrational. The second concept of autonomy is distinct from 'rationality/irrationality' because whereas the former is essentially a tool for discussing the *authorship* of beliefs, desires, emotions and actions, the latter is primarily a tool for facilitating disputes about their *acceptability*.

This does not entail that the two concepts refer to different objects. Indeed, one view about agency is that an agent is autonomous if and only if she is rational. On this view, in other words, although autonomy and rationality are *formally* distinct concepts, they are *co-extensive*. This is a key doctrine of 'the Kantian view'.

The Kantian view

For Kant the most important fact about people, from the moral point of view, is that we are creatures with a will. Because we are able to act for the sake of principles we have set for ourselves, freedom, and therefore moral responsibility, is possible. Non-human animals may have appetites or drives, which motivate them to act in a purposive way, but, with the possible exception of some mammals, they act simply in accordance with instinct. Driver ants march in long columns. When they reach a stream, those at the head just march into the water and drown, with no thought for their own safety. Eventually, the pile of corpses is large enough to enable those behind to cross, thus ensuring the survival of the colony. The unsung heroes do not, however, deserve medals for extreme courage in the cause of their community, because they have no choice. They simply behave in this manner. Non-rational creatures are incapable of choice, and therefore of moral virtue.

Although non-rational creatures lack the capacity for choice, they can be subject to appetites. They look for food and drink, defend themselves against attack, protect their young, have sex, and participate in many activities also pursued by people. If the capacity to engage in such pursuits is something which people share with non-rational animals, it cannot be through the indulgence of such appetites alone that we have a will.

To possess a will, a creature must have the capacity to act in a way which is not dictated by immediate inclination. People are able to reflect on feelings or inclinations which they may have at a particular time, and may decide to act contrary to the push of inclination. I may feel like having another drink, and yet refuse as a result of my reasoning that one more drink would leave me with a headache in the morning.

The will is really the faculty of choice. Thus someone's will is not identical with any one desire, or even a strongest desire. A person's will in a given practical context is what he finally resolves to do. The function of practical reason is to affect the reasoner's behaviour by changing her will. When somebody makes an offensive remark in a meeting my inclination is to storm out. However, as a result of reasoning about the situation I decide to resist the inclination. I realise that it would be pointless to leave; for this would help nobody, and would likely defeat my purposes in attending the meeting. If reason is seen as the faculty which enables creatures with a will to make the best choices, it is a small step to characterise as 'irrational', the non-optimal actions of a will. This is why 'irrationality' is the most general and fundamental charge which can be levelled against a creature with a will. The Kantian view includes a distinctive account of rationality, and equates rationality with autonomy. I shall now say something about the former.

Pure rationality

In order to resist the charge of imperfect rationality, it is necessary for an agent's motives to be untainted by inclination. Inclinations come and go, according to the vagaries of our physical constitutions and experiences. In so far as our behaviour is determined by inclinations we are not acting fully rationally. To be fully rational is to be motivated by rationality alone. What can this mean?

If my aim is to be a successful candidate in an election, it is rational for me to mobilise support in the community. The role of reason here is to find appropriate means for the realisation of my ends. But what of the ends? Suppose I have as an end, total world supremacy, as perhaps Adolf Hitler once had. It might be rational, given that end, for me to perpetrate numerous atrocities, and to become a manipulator and tyrant. Someone might not be able to fault my effectiveness in the pursuit of this goal, but still wish to condemn me as irrational, for having such an irrational end. On the view in question, to be fully rational (i.e. fully autonomous), one's ends, as well as means, must be purely rational.

To understand 'purely rational motivation' it is useful to

consider an analogy with 'purely rational belief'. What do you have reason to believe? In part this depends on where you are situated in the world. For beliefs depend on evidence, and evidence, say about the street crime problem in New York, which is available to a New Yorker, may be unavailable to a citizen of New Delhi. The truth about the crime rate in New York is not a truth of reason, because people may have different beliefs on the subject, without this suggesting that either party must be irrational. Rationality alone does not deliver any situation-specific beliefs. On the other hand, laws of logic, such as the law of non-contradiction (which states that no proposition and its contradiction can be *both* true together), could be called truths of reason. Any rational person should recognise the truth of the law of non-contradiction, irrespective of where she or he is located in the world. It is universal in form, since it holds of *any* proposition and its contradiction. It binds all rational creatures.

Now consider two people – a New Yorker and a New Delhian – sitting on an international committee which administers poverty relief. Suppose that money from the committee could go to relieve poverty either in New York, or in New Delhi, but not both. The New Yorker feels worse about New York poverty, whereas the New Delhian feels worse about that in his home city. How should they vote to distribute the aid? In so far as their reasons are determined by their feelings, by what they would like to happen, they will vote in opposite ways. It is possible for two rational people to have feeling-based reasons to *do* opposite things, just as it is possible for two rational people to have perception-based reasons to *believe* opposite things. Both are 'situation-specific'.

'Purely rational motivation' is analogous to 'purely rational belief' in that purely rational reasons for action (if there are any) apply to all creatures with a will simply in virtue of their rationality. They are, then, not situation-specific, and cannot be reasons provided by sectional interests, nor by particular inclinations. For it is possible for people to have conflicting reasons of *this* sort without it following that at least one party is irrational.

Just as purely rational beliefs should be *believed* by all, so purely rational motivating principles should be *willed* by all. A purely rational principle of action is one which binds any creature with a will, irrespective of the vagaries of their own particular circumstances. The best way to test whether a principle of your own is of this type is to ask whether you could will that it be universally followed. If you could will this, then you may rest (reasonably) assured that the principle does not derive its force from the particularities of your own situation. Kant calls an action-guiding principle of this form a *categorical* imperative, as opposed to merely *hypothetical* imperatives, because its force is not contingent on the particular goals of the people to whom it applies. It applies to everyone, that is, all people, and any other creatures with a will that there may be. Kant's first formulation of the categorical imperative is:

'Act only on that maxim through which you can at the same time will that it should become a universal law.' (Kant, 1785, p.84)

This is a second-order principle – a principle for testing principles. It requires people to act only on principles of a certain form – namely principles which are universal in the sense that the agent can will that the principles become universal, followed by all people at all times. If the New Yorker and the New Delhian were each able to adhere to the categorial imperative, they would not have conflicting goals, since the conflict is due to the fact that each is motivated by sectional interest. Those following the categorical imperative will be motivated by concern for the interests of all those affected by their conduct, including those about whom they don't care emotionally; for they would want their own interests to be protected, and pure practical rationality allows no special weight to be given to situation–specific facts (There is nothing special, from a purely rational point of view, about interests or concerns being *mine*).

One objection sometimes raised against this is that it *is* possible for someone to will that his own interests be disregarded. If there could be such creatures, then principles which require one to respect impartially the interests of all, would not be properly universalisable; but merely universalisable for some. Kant thought there could not be such creatures, because he believed that all rational creatures desire their own well-being; but even if there could be, the principle (of showing impartial respect for the interests of all) would retain its force at least for those who *would* not will that their own interests were disregarded – which is probably the vast majority of people.

The worth of people

Goods in the market have a price; but what price should be put on the heads of people? According to the Kantian view no price *can* be put on people, because, being creatures with a will, we have plans and projects of our own. We are therefore the originators of value. The value of goods is a function of how useful they might be as means to the ends of their owners. Because we are the *authors* of plans and projects our worth is on a different plane from things, which have value only in so far as they are useful for the pursuit of plans and projects. Kant wrote:

> 'Rational nature exists as an end in itself. This is the way in which a man necessarily conceives his own existence: it is therefore so far a *subjective* principle of human actions. But it is also the way in which every other rational being conceives his existence on the same rational ground which is valid also for me; hence it is at the same time an *objective* principle, from which, as a supreme practical ground, it must be possible to derive all laws for the will. The practical imperative will therefore be as follows: Act in such a way that you always treat humanity, whether in your own person or in the person of any other, never simply as a means, but always at the same time as an end.' (Ibid., p.91)

To summarise: According to what I have called the Kantian view, to be fully autonomous is equivalent to being a fully rational agent. To be a fully rational agent is to be motivated by purely rational principles, which are untainted by particular inclinations or interests. Such purity requires that one act only on principles one is prepared to universalise in a strong sense. This in turn requires that one treat all human beings never simply as means to ends, but as ends in themselves (because it is impossible for a creature with a will to regard itself simply as a means to an end).

What is wrong with the human farming experiment described at the beginning of this chapter? According to the Kantian view, and I think the liberal democratic tradition, its main problem is that it fails to treat all people as creatures which have their own projects and goals. The Kantian view has much to commend it, but is also open to objections, some of which I shall now discuss.

Rationality and authorship

I claimed at the beginning of this chapter that the concepts of rationality and autonomy were indeed separate because, whilst autonomy is primarily a matter of authorship, rationality is essentially a matter of acceptability. The charge 'irrational' is the most general criticism of creatures with a will. To be heteronomous is to be out of internal control of one's own life. The Kantian view does not entail that autonomy and rationality are the same concept; merely that they are co-extensive.

Even this weaker claim is questionable, most obviously if one accepts the Kantian view of rationality. Autonomy is self-rule. Thus, whether or not a person is an autonomous agent is a function of the connection between his self and his actions. He is autonomous to the extent that his actions emanate from his self, as opposed either to the will of another, or from something internal other than his self. To have a self is to have a fairly settled character. A character is, amongst other things, a disposition to think, feel and act according to one's unique view of the world. We thus speak of a person's 'characteristics', of acting 'in character', and so on.

For an agent to act autonomously, her action must emanate from her will. Why should one assume that the 'true' will of all agents is purely rational, that is, not subject to individual quirks or biases or inclinations? Suppose a father loves his son. Faced with a choice between giving his son a birthday present, and contributing to a fund for fighting starvation in Ethiopia, he opts for the former. This choice could not plausibly derive from a principle which the father would will to be a universal law. Hence it fails the Kantian test for rationality. But there doesn't appear to be a good reason for supposing that it fails to emanate from the will of the father. He may be acting autonomously. So autonomy and Kantian rationality seem to be anything but co-extensive. Why ever might someone think they were?

Autonomy, freedom and responsibility

If nobody were ever morally responsible for their actions, it would not make sense to speak of people *deserving* rewards or punishments for their conduct. Yet the belief that people do have such deserts is very pervasive, especially in societies within the Judaeo/Christian religious tradition. The threat of divine retribution and the promise of heavenly rewards have been amongst the most powerful social organisers, encouraging people to accept prevalent social norms of the societies in which they happen to live. Even in post-religious society the belief that people genuinely have deserts remains a strong force for maintaining social order.

The belief that people are, or may be, morally responsible for their actions, is difficult to square with the belief that all events in the world are naturally determined. Kant believed that human desires or appetites are caused by events in the world. Each event, including the event of coming to have a desire, is but one link in a causal chain, which extends both forwards, through an indefinite number of consequences, and backwards, beyond the person having the desire. Given all the antecedent events in the world, whenever someone has a desire or inclination, he or she could not but have it. Thus, if I am moved to pity a beggar before me, although this might lead me to do the right thing, coming to have pity is not *morally* praiseworthy, because, given the state of the world, it was, independently of my will, inevitable that I would feel pity. Those who are susceptible to pity do not *deserve* rewards for feeling pity, any more than people deserve to be punished for being by nature unsympathetic. People are, on this view, simply beset by feelings.

If moral responsibility, and therefore moral desert, is to be possible, there has to be human motivation which is not just naturally determined. Moreover, this motivation must be attributable to the people who are allegedly responsible. Kant believed that pure practical reason was suitable for this role – of explaining how moral responsibility, and therefore, Christian morality, might be possible.

As people have all sorts of feelings or inclinations, which come upon them through being in certain places at certain times, principles of conduct which are the product of these inclinations, are not due to the self alone. For, on this view, the substantial self is that which remains constant throughout these changes. Actions performed through pursuit of such principles (of inclination) are *heteronomous*. On the other hand, the principles of reason are universal. All people, irrespective of where they come from, how they feel, or what they believe, ought to follow the principles of reason. The 'I ought to do this', which is the conclusion of practical reasoning, is according to Kant, the voice of the deliberator's own self. For it to be an authentic expression, the practical judgment has to be untainted by non-essential trappings, such as particular inclinations. Only then is the deliberator truly autonomous – that is, motivated by principles which derive from his own self alone. To be autonomous is to act on self-chosen principles. The self is essentially a rational self. We are all bound by the principles of rationality; but this is the key to our freedom and responsibility, since these principles are the principles of our own nature.

There are many problems with this Kantian account, two of which I shall discuss here. (For a fuller discussion see Wolff, 1973, Chapter 3, and Bennett, 1974, Chapter 10.)

One internal difficulty of this account as an attempt to make sense of moral responsibility and traditional beliefs about moral desert is that it apparently entails that people are morally responsible only for actions which are performed through purely rational principles. A person may, from time to time, do the right thing out of inclination, rather than for the sake of purely rational (self-prescribed) principles. This, as Kant argues in the case of the grocer who honestly gives a child correct change in order best to promote his business, nullifies any *moral* worth the action may have. The grocer does not deserve moral praise for his conduct, because it does not derive from the principles of his own rational will. He is not autonomous, so the good deed is not properly attributable to him. But if this reasoning is acceptable, then we should not be morally responsible for our wrongdoing, in so far as wrongdoing is action motivated by self-centred inclination. Kant himself clearly believed that we are responsible for our numerous sins (see his *Religion Within the Limits of Reason Alone*), but it is hard to understand how, in the end, this is consistent with the view that we are morally praiseworthy only if our motives are rationally pure. For this would require that, *from a purely rational motive*, one could decide to act wickedly; but the source of wickedness on this view is inclination. If one person *could* choose to be wicked on purely rational principles, then so *should* all rational creatures, which, on Kant's own view, is absurd.

The most serious deficiency of the account is that it is quite unintelligible how the causality of the rational self is supposed to relate to events in the world. People's deliberations take place within the same spatio-temporal order as other natural events in the world. The thoughts that people have at any time, and the reasoning in which they will engage, is determined by the state of their central nervous system and their environment at that time. There is no reason to suppose that the deliberations of pure practical reason are any less caused by brain events than are those of inclination-tainted deliberation. Moreover, if it were the case that there is a natural causal order, which includes the actions of bodies (including human bodies), as well as the coming and going of inclinations, it is difficult to see how the 'actions' of the rational self could, if they do anything, fail to violate the laws of the natural causal order. If they did this, then the causal order would not, properly-speaking, be a causal order at all.

The fact that people are sometimes moved by principles which appeal to all rational creatures, independently of their particular circumstances, does not entail that when they are so moved, the event of their being moved takes place out of time, or that there are not particular naturally caused circumstances which led them to be moved in that way at that time.

I think the main reason for equating pure rationality with autonomy stems from the conflation of moral responsibility for action with autonomy, combined with the belief that a person is morally responsible only for those of his actions which are not caused by inclination.

People are *causally* responsible for the consequences of their actions; some of their actions, though not others, are intentional; some are manifestations of good or ill-will towards people; it is natural to resent or be grateful for some conduct; society would change, perhaps out of all recognition if we stopped holding people responsible for their actions. But none of this shows that anybody ever *is*, morally responsible for their conduct. Although here is not the place to argue the case in detail, I believe that nobody *is* ever morally responsible in the sense which would give them pure deserts (for an argument along these lines see Honderich, 1973). However, such a rejection of moral responsibility does not entail a rejection of the possibility of autonomy. In fact, if autonomy can be distinguished from the sort of freedom from causal determination which is thought to be necessary to explain moral desert, it becomes easier to see how autonomy might *be* possible.

If autonomy is self-rule, then the extent to which an agent is autonomous is determined by the relation of the *nomos* of her conduct to herself. Consider, for example, someone who had been hypnotised to carry out the will of another. When the hypnotist snaps his finger, in accordance with a hypnotic suggestion the subject picks up a pin, and sticks it into his wrist. He is not acting autonomously, since his will is being controlled by another. Whatever rationale there is for sticking the pin in his wrist does not emanate from his own purposes. The reasons for the pin-sticker's behaviour are not his own, and may be quite inconsistent with his own purposes. Next consider an infant who has no recognisable set of goals, who has no conception of the long, or even medium-term. She follows her immediate inclinations, except where prevented by outside obstacles. *She* is not autonomous, because there is not yet a developed self which *could* provide the principle of conduct.

The above two examples of lack of autonomy suggest that there are ways in which the world could be so structured that people are causally determined to become autonomous. If a person's genetic endowment is right, and he is brought up in a congenial environment he may develop a character which enables him to become autonomous. The reasons for action of an autonomous person may be attributable to that person – to his inner core, unless, as for example in the case of the hypnotist's subject, there is an external directing principle. Whether autonomy is possible is a function of genetics and environment, and is independent of the question of whether there might be purely rational, non-naturally-determined motivation. Even if every event in the universe is determined, the causal history of some events may be such that part of their explanation requires reference to the (relatively) autonomous decisions of agents. Instead of equating autonomy with moral responsibility we should speak of some people's causal history's being such that they have been able to develop and exercise autonomy, whilst that of others renders *them* less fortunate.

It is wrong to equate pure rationality with autonomy because there is no reason to suppose that the self has to be a purely rational self, unmoved by particular interests. However, it is plausible to claim that irrationality is contrary to autonomy, and therefore that rationality is a necessary condition for autonomy. If someone arrives at a decision through bad reasoning, it is a matter of luck whether the decision best promotes his fundamental projects. This is reflected in the different attitudes it is appropriate to take towards those who injure us knowing full well what they are doing, and towards those who, through irrationality, are unaware of the nature of their actions. Irrationality is an obstacle, perhaps the most widespread and important obstacle, to being in control of one's conduct.

For this reason, any account of autonomy needs to include a conception of rationality. The Kantian conception of rationality entails that it is irrational to be motivated by any specific attachments, or biases. We always have most reason to act on principles which we can will to be universal laws. This view is questionable.

Reasons and emotions

It may be quite true that if someone adopted a standard of 'pure rationality' this would entail a commitment to placing no special weight on her own desires and commitments. For looked at neutrally, my suffering or pleasure, the avoidance or promotion of which *I* desire, is no more important or valuable than anyone else's, which *they* desire. The special weight I attach to my own well-being, and to that of those near and dear to me is, from the perspective of 'pure reason' a bias. But why *should* someone, who does not want to, adopt this neutral position? In order for the view to have any force, it has to be able to support the thesis not just that adopting universalisable principles is a requirement of *pure* rationality, but that any deviation from the standard of pure rationality is itself irrational; and this thesis is not so easy to defend. The most celebrated classical statement of the rival opinion to the Kantian view of rationality comes from David Hume. According to him, it is impossible for reason alone to motivate – a passion or desire is also required. Furthermore, Hume claims that passions themselves are neither rational nor irrational. Hence there are, on his view, no categorical imperatives, since what someone has most reason to do is determined directly by his or her goals, which in turn are fixed by non-rational passions, which may vary from person to person, without implying that at least one of the parties is irrational.

Conclusion

The Kantian view could be described as an extreme rationalist conception of autonomy, since it claims that rationality is not merely necessary, but also sufficient for autonomy, and identifies rationality (the avoidance of irrationality) with pure rationality (being untainted by desire or inclination).

I have argued, against Kant, that rationality and autonomy are not co-extensive; pure rationality does not deliver moral responsibility; and anyway actions can be properly attributable to people who are not purely rational. Whereas it is right that irrationality is an obstacle to autonomy, it is not at all clear that the avoidance of irrationality requires an agent to be purely rational in Kant's sense.

The most important contribution to liberal theory of the Kantian view is the principle of equal respect for individual people, which is based on a recognition that people are (equally) creatures with a will. Although the conception of what it is to be self-governing may be mistaken in its extreme rationalism, the ideal of moral autonomy is of vital significance to liberal theory, as will become evident later in the book. It is a theme taken up in particular by Mill.

But now I turn to discussion of a Humean conception of autonomy, in many respects diametrically opposed to the Kantian.

3 The Destruction of the Whole World

"'Tis not contrary to reason to prefer the destruction of the whole world to the scratching of my finger.' (Hume, 1739)

I have claimed that the Kantian identification of autonomy with pure rationality is mistaken, although rationality is a necessary condition for autonomy. To be autonomous is to act on self-chosen principles. Rationality is, at least, the faculty which enables a person to make the best use of his ability to choose, and someone who makes better use of this ability is more in control of his decisions than a person who uses it less well. So any conception of autonomy requires its own view of rationality. Indeed, one of the key disagreements between different theories of autonomy is over the proper role of reason in the determination of desire and action. The central focus of this chapter will be a conception of autonomy which I have derived from David Hume, and is most noteworthy for its distinctive theory of rationality.

A theory of rationality is supposed to deliver a decision-making procedure for telling people what they have most reason to do, believe, want or feel. According to the Kantian view everyone has most reason to act in an impartial way, guided by purely rational considerations, which are untainted by inclinations or feelings. Thus, in deciding what to do, a person is asked to set aside all personal considerations which derive from what she in particular wants or cherishes. In Chapter 2 I claimed that the Kantian argument for such a view is less than convincing. Hume was one of the strongest opponents of this view, even though his writing on the subject predates Kant's.

The ultimate ends of human action

The clearest statement of Hume's view of rationality is in Book II, Part III, section III, and Book III, Part I, section I of *A Treatise of Human Nature*. He begins the former by declaring his opposition to a traditional view of the human condition, which was accepted by Kant – namely that human life consists of a never-ending struggle between our reason and our passions. This view is associated with the idea that motivation by passion is base, whereas motivation by reason alone, is elevated. Speaking of this traditional view Hume writes:

> 'In order to shew the fallacy of all this philosophy, I shall endeavour to prove *first*, that reason alone can never be a motive to any action of the will; and *secondly*, that it can never oppose passion in the direction of the will.' (Hume, 1739, p.413)

For a detailed analysis of Hume's argument I refer the reader to Stroud, 1977, Chapter VII. I shall offer a sketch, since once again, my prime aim is not scholarly exegesis, but the discussion of a position – in this case a position which owes more to Hume than to any other thinker.

Hume identifies reason with the understanding. It is the faculty which provides us with information about the world. The knowledge which reason enables us to acquire is either *a priori* knowledge of necessary truths, or *a posteriori* knowledge of empirical probabilities. In both cases, Hume argues, the knowledge we acquire is insufficient to provide motivation on its own. For example, I might realise, as a result of careful deliberation, that a likely effect of my failure to repair the brake pipes on the presidential limousine is that the president will be killed. This may motivate me to repair them – if I do not want to be responsible for the president's death; but on the other hand, if I wanted his death it might equally motivate me to do and say nothing. In the absence of controls, the discovery that using lead shot in my angling endangers the life of swans is likely to persuade me to use alternative weights, only if I care about the fate of swans. Reasoning about the effects of my conduct helps me better to pursue my goals; but in order for the reasoning to be efficacious I must have preferences or desires which set the goals for the pursuit of which the information provided by reason is to be used. The crucial question is whether preferences or desires can themselves be produced by reason alone. Hume's view is that they cannot. This is because, according to him, the 'affections' which stir us into action are 'original existences', not representative of reality (as beliefs are), hence incapable of being true or false, and therefore beyond the scope of rational criticism. In fact he *does* allow the rational criticism of affections which are founded on false beliefs, but, he writes:

> 'Where a passion is neither founded on false suppositions nor chuses means insufficient for the design'd end, the understanding [i.e. reason] can neither justify nor condemn it.' (Ibid., p.416)

There are three categories of rational evaluation. A belief, desire, feeling or action may be rationally *required*, rationally *permitted*, or rationally *proscribed*. Hume's view of desires, feelings and actions, amounts to the claim that, unless they derive from false beliefs, they are all rationally permissible. To stress the point in a way people would not forget Hume wrote:

> ''Tis not contrary to reason to prefer the destruction of the whole world to the scratching of my finger. 'Tis not contrary to reason for me to chuse my total ruin, to prevent the least uneasiness of an Indian [sic!] or person wholly unknown to me. 'Tis as little contrary to reason to prefer even my own acknowledg'd lesser good to my greater, and have a more ardent affection for the former than the latter.' (Ibid., p.416)

Whereas Kant's theory presents reason as the rightful governor of the person, which has, as it were, to resist the anarchic insubordination of sentiments, Hume describes reason as 'the slave of the passions'. This is, however, an overstatement of his own position, which is more that reason's relation to sentiments is like the official relation between a civil service and an elected government. Civil servants are supposed to provide ministers with information about the likely consequences of the various options which are put before them. Government would be impossible without this service; however, the policy decisions are taken by the government, not the civil service, in line with the objectives of the former. We all know the strength of civil servants' influence on government, but as long as a policy decision is not taken in ignorance, it is beyond the professional role of a civil servant to praise or condemn it.

The crucial disagreement between Kantian and Humean is over the role of reason in dictating sound policy objectives for the self. For Kant the sole seat of self-government is the faculty of reason. For Hume there are two branches of government – the sentiments which fix an agent's ultimate ends, and reason which administers the pursuit of these ends as efficiently as possible. Thus Hume writes about fundamental goals, in the First Appendix to his *Enquiry Concerning the Principles of Morals*:

'It appears evident that the ultimate ends of human actions can never, in any case, be accounted for by *reason*, but recommend themselves entirely to the sentiments and affections of mankind, without any dependance on the intellectual faculties. . . . It is impossible there can be a progress *in infinitum*; and that one thing can always be a reason why another is desired. Something must be desirable on its own account, and because of its immediate accord or agreement with human sentiment and affection.' (Hume, 1751, p.293)

If an agent were rationally required to have and pursue an end this would restrict the choice of options consistent with his autonomy. For autonomy requires a person not to be irrational, and failing to adopt a policy which is rationally *required* is irrational. A deliberating agent who accepts the Kantian view of rationality may feel greatly restricted. On that view one is required to overrule the promptings of particular desires and feelings, even overall preferences, all in the name of a strict impartiality. Anything less is irrational. The Humean view, by contrast, is comparatively easy on the agent. The fact that someone has a set of projects which cannot be justified by appeal to impartial principles in no way implies that it would be irrational for her to pursue them. On the other hand, someone who wants to live solely in accordance with Kantian principles is, as far as the principles of Humean rationality are concerned, perfectly at liberty to do so. Hume had a minimalist conception of rationality. But what of autonomy?

Autonomy and freedom

Although Hume did not write about autonomy by name, it is possible to construct a Humean view of autonomy, by drawing not only on his writings on rationality, but also on his account of free will. For like Kant, he was interested in the problem of how genuine human agency could be possible in a causally ordered world, and to this discussion I now turn.

Much of Kant's moral philosophy was a response to the threat to conventional Christian morality, which he saw in determinism. Because he thought that complete causal determination was inconsistent with free action, he was driven to postulate the possibility of a kind of causality which operated independently of the determined world of nature. This was the supposed purely rational motivation of the inclination-free autonomous will. Nobody has properly made sense of this special kind of causation.

Hume avoided the problem, I think for two reasons. First, he was prepared to countenance the view that conventional morality may be mistaken. He wrote:

'There is no method of reasoning more common, and yet none more blameable than in philosophical debates to endeavour to refute any hypothesis by a pretext of its dangerous consequences to religion and morality. When any opinion leads us into absurdities, 'tis certainly false; but 'tis not certain an opinion is false, because 'tis of dangerous consequence.' (Hume, 1739, p.409)

Second, he believed that determinism was perfectly compatible with 'liberty', as he calls it. His solution to the problem is delightfully simple. He diagnoses the source of the so-called 'free-will problem' as the result of a linguistic confusion. We talk of 'liberty' and 'necessity', and suppose the two are mutually incompatible. However, the true opposite of 'liberty' is 'compulsion', whereas the true opposite of 'necessity' is 'chance' or 'randomness'. Hume argues that all events we can explain, including human actions, are 'necessary' in the sense that they do not occur at random. For Hume 'necessity' in this context meant 'predictability' and 'regularity'. Human conduct is no more nor less regular than the behaviour of phenomena in the non-human

world. In fact Hume believed that such 'necessity' is a precondition
of 'liberty' (see Hume, 1739, p.411). But what, then, is 'liberty'?

'Liberty' is contrasted with 'compulsion'. A person is not at
liberty if he is being forced against his will. Hume's clearest
statement of the nature of 'liberty' is in the *Enquiry Concerning
the Human Understanding*.

> 'By liberty, then, we can only mean *a power of acting or not
> acting, according to the determinations of the will*; that is, if we
> choose to remain at rest we may; if we choose to move, we also
> may. Now this hypothetical liberty is universally allowed to
> belong to every one who is not a prisoner and in chains. Here,
> then, is no subject of dispute.' (Hume, 1748, p.95)

If, in the above, we were to substitute the word 'autonomy' for
'liberty', we would have the second key strand of what I call the
'Humean view' of autonomy. Whereas on the Kantian view, you
have to be unusually conscientious to be autonomous, on the
Humean view, you have to be unusually careless or unlucky to
fail to be autonomous. The Humean view relegates reason to a
subordinate role in the proper determination of action. For any
preference is rationally permissible provided it is not founded on
'false suppositions', and to be autonomous is simply to act on
those of your rationally permissible desires, which most take your
fancy – to do as you choose.

In the last chapter I argued that the Kantian conception was
too restrictive. The major criticism levelled against a Humean
conception of rationality, and hence of autonomy, is that it is too
permissive. I shall consider this alleged failing; but first it is
necessary to amend Hume's own view of rationality to avoid
obvious, but for our present concerns, irrelevant objections, to
the Humean view of autonomy.

Deliberation

Hume actually wrote that passions are subject to rational criticism
only if they are founded on 'false suppositions'. In order to make
his theory plausible this needs amendment. There is a gap
between rationality of belief and truth, although rational beliefs

are those arrived at by generally reliable methods. If, through no fault of my own, I have been deceived, say by the weather forecast warning that a hurricane is about to hit my town, it may be rational for me to believe that it is dangerous to return home, whereas in fact there is no danger. Under these circumstances my fear of returning home is based on a false supposition, but it is not irrational. Similarly, it is possible irrationally to hold a belief which turns out true. Hume should have said that passions are subject to rational criticism only if they derive from *irrational* beliefs, arrived at or sustained through inadequate deliberation.

According to the revised Humean view, then, rational actions are simply those which are the result of proper deliberation about the nature and consequences of possible lines of conduct. For if all actions are the product of a motivating passion, and passions can be irrational only if they stem from irrational beliefs, then it is only at the stage of deliberation that irrationality can creep in. But what is 'proper deliberation'? It is remarkably difficult to specify. In several recent discussions of rationality philosophers such as Brandt (1979) and Parfit (1984) have equated 'proper deliberation' with what they call 'ideal deliberation'. Parfit discusses a view of rationality, called by him the 'Deliberative Theory', which captures the Humean idea that irrationality is a failure in belief formation.

> 'What each of us has most reason to do is what would best achieve, not what he *actually* wants, but what he *would* want, at the time of acting, if he had undergone a process of "ideal deliberation" – if he knew the relevant facts, was thinking clearly, and was free from distorting influences.' (Parfit, 1984, p.118)

As what we want very often differs from what we would want were we to have undergone 'ideal deliberation', the Deliberative Theory places severe restrictions on the desires which may, without our being irrational, motivate us. There are at least two difficulties with this theory.

First, even Parfit's clear formulation leaves a number of controversial terms undefined, and it is difficult to offer adequate interpretations of these terms. For instance, how are we to delimit 'relevant facts'? Parfit, whilst admitting that his definition needs refinement, refrains from offering one because it is not required for *his* purposes, which are to reject the Deliberative Theory on other grounds. He states that 'The relevant facts are those of which it is true that, if this person knew this fact, his desires would change. Whilst it is true that relevant facts do make a difference, it is not obvious that all facts the consideration of which would make a difference to decisions are relevant in any plausible sense, to what a deliberating agent has most reason to do. Suppose someone suffers from psychogenic allergic reactions. He is allergic to cat hair, but only when he is aware of the fact that there are hairs in his vicinity. He is spending a very enjoyable evening at a friend's house, unaware that the friend has a cat. Had he realised that a cat lived at this house, he would form the desire to leave. This does not mean that he actually has more reason to leave than to stay, or that his decision to stay is in any way irrational. There are similar problems with 'thinking clearly' and 'distorting influence'.

The second, and perhaps fatal, flaw in the Deliberative Theory, for those sympathetic to a Humean view about the rational permissibility of ultimate ends, lies in its insistence that what the agent has most reason to do depends on *hypothetical* wants. If someone were to think more clearly, and not be subject to ideological distortion of values, this might dramatically affect what she wants. Take the case of a woman who has accepted the traditional role of women as mother and housekeeper. You realise that if she could free herself from these distorted beliefs she would no longer want just to marry, settle down and have a family, but would prefer to go to college, and seek financial independence. Does she have more reason to go to college, or to settle down? On the Deliberative Theory it appears that she has more reason to go to college, whether or not she does the deliberating which would change her desires. It might be rational for this person to go to college, even though she really does not want to go, and would hate every minute of life at college. For ideal deliberation may not just change some specific wants for things as supposed means to desired ends, but may affect a person's whole wanting constitution, which is the repository of her interests. Given her cognitive limitations she obviously has more reason not to go to college. The aim of practical deliberation is to make the best decision. Even if someone realised that if he considered all relevant information he would prefer x to y, it does not follow that he has most reason to choose x. If, as things stand, he prefers y, y may represent, for him, the better choice. It is an open question whether it would be rational to engage in the further deliberations which would lead to the change in preference. Suppose someone realised that if he considered all relevant information about the human condition this would drive him to suicide. This does not mean that he has more reason to kill himself than to continue his quite pleasant life. In this respect desires are different from beliefs. If I reason that, were I to consider all the evidence and think clearly, I would come to *believe x*, this gives me reason to believe x, whether or not I do consider all the evidence. (The topic of hypothetical preferences is taken up again in discussions about people's real interests, in Chapters 4 and 10.)

Consideration of the Deliberative Theory highlights the importance of a distinction between what someone has most reason to do, given her actual set of preferences and goals, and what set of preferences and goals it would be most rational for her to acquire or retain. It may be possible to embark on strategies for changing one's own patterns of preference. Consider, for example, Buddhist meditation. An aim of this practice is to free the meditator from craving for the permanence of the evanescent objects of desire. What is rational for me to do after I have gained Buddhist enlightenment may be radically different from what is rational before. Whether or not to engage in meditation is a genuine, substantive question. Is it rational for me to engage in Buddhist meditation? Is it rational for me to engage in ideal deliberation? According to the Deliberative Theory, whether or not it is rational is determined by what I would prefer had I *undergone* this deliberation. But unless I am actually going to undergo this process, it is not clear that the hypothetical preferences I would have are relevant to the rationality of any choice I might make.

The revised Humean theory of rationality, which I shall consider for the rest of this chapter, and shall refer to simply as the 'Humean theory', is essentially a theory about which preferences or desires a person has most reason to acquire or retain. It states that any preferences or desires are rationally permissible, unless they are the product of defective deliberation.

The onus is put on the critic to state wherein lies the error in the reasoning, which is responsible for the preferences of the subject of the criticism. This theory can be applied to individual cases without references to a definitive standard of *ideal* deliberation.

The ideal of Kantian rationality is someone who is motivated by purely rational considerations – there is no place for particular likes and dislikes. The ideal of the Deliberative Theory is pure *theoretical* rationality – that people be motivated by the preferences they would have were they purely theoretically rational. The Humean theory is distinctive, in that it has minimal ideals. What a person has most reason to do is determined by his actual desires and preferences. If a preference is sustained through irrational beliefs, then the person has reason to change the preference. But the preferences he would have, were he purely theoretically rational, are not directly relevant to what is rational for him to do. Similarly, the choices he would make, were he free of all partiality, are equally irrelevant to what he has most reason to do.

On the Humean view an autonomous individual pursues the life of his choice, chasing as efficiently as possible the goals set by his non-rational preferences. At the point when he reaches the age of deliberation, what is most rational for him to do is determined by the preferences he then has. The choices he makes will then affect what comes to be rational for him to do, not least of all, by generating new sets of preferences. I shall consider two lines of attack on the Humean theory – one from a Kantian direction, the other from a position which rejects this Kantian criticism.

Neutrality

Hume claimed that it is not irrational to 'prefer my own acknowledg'd lesser good to my greater'. A prime case of this would be someone who is knowingly imprudent. You point out to him that his present over-indulgence will damage his health, thus making his long-term life prospects worse overall. He agrees with you, but states that he simply does not care that much about his future. Let us assume that his imprudence is not based on a false assessment of what the future will hold for him, since even a

Humean could condemn *that* as irrational. Why, then, might prudence be rationally required of this person? One reason for believing this is that reason is supposed to be impartial – to avoid making arbitrary distinctions.

Suppose that I have a headache, this gives me a reason to eliminate the pain. Why? Because pain is awful. But its awfulness is not a function of the time at which it occurs, but rather of its intensity and duration. If it is the awfulness of the pain which provides me with the reason for taking a pain-killer then, unless I am to be guilty of arbitrary, and therefore irrational inconsistency, I should acknowledge a reason to prevent anything awful. My future pains are, in principle I may suppose, no less awful than present ones. For the experiences I shall come to have are no less real (and potentially awful) than my present experiences. Of course the future is uncertain, and this makes it rational to discount future pains somewhat, but any further discounting is irrational.

Hume also claimed, in dramatic fashion as we have seen, that it is not irrational to be thoroughly selfish, preferring the total ruin of everyone else, in order to avoid a tiny suffering for oneself. Such a preference may be immoral, but why should it be thought irrational? First, as with gross imprudence, it is likely that anyone with such a preference would be deluded – unaware of what his preference really meant. However, were *this* the cause of the preference, it would be subject even to Humean rational criticism.

The neutrality argument proceeds in a similar way to that for prudence. Just as the awfulness of pain is not a function of *when* it occurs, so it is not a function of *to whom* it occurs. If I am motivated to care about my own well-being, but care nothing for others, I am treating them as if their lives and experiences are less real than my own. But, unless I am a solipsist I do not believe this. So lack of altruism is irrational, because it is a kind of inconsistency. (For a full exposition and defence of these arguments see Nagel, 1970.)

At first (and perhaps even second) sight, these arguments seem persuasive. However, all I am actually committed to by a recognition of the reality of other people's suffering is that they too have reasons to prevent their own suffering. It does not follow that I am irrational if I do not seek to prevent their suffering. Similarly, I might well fully recognise the reality of my future without caring about it. The generality of reasons commits me to recognising that in the future, I shall have reasons to wish that earlier I had been more prudent, which will be no less strong than reasons given by present desires for a good time now. However, it does not *commit* me (on pain of irrationality) to caring equally about all stages of my life. The reasons which I act on are reasons which *I* have *now*. Prudence and altruism are certainly required by strict neutrality, but it is hard to show that strict neutrality is required by reason. To have and act on biases towards the present or towards myself, does not render me guilty of inconsistency. The Humean view can survive the attack from the alleged neutrality of reasons.

Irrational desires

According to the Humean theory all desires provide some reason for action, and the stronger the desire the stronger the reason. This requires acceptance of the claim that no desires are what I shall call 'essentially irrational', that is, subject to rational criticism even though they are neither produced nor sustained by irrational beliefs. On this view irrationality is simply a function of the relation between belief and reasons for belief. What a person has most reason to *do* is just a function of the desires and preferences he has at the time.

The Humean view of the rational thing to do is, however, still vulnerable, even if it can withstand the attack from neutrality. For the rejection of neutralism about rationality entails neither that there are no essentially irrational desires, nor that the only role of reason in *action* is ensuring that there are no irrational beliefs in the deliberative process.

These two claims – about essentially irrational desires, and about the role of reason in action – are distinct. I shall defend the former, and reject the latter.

Many desires are irrational. A mentally ill person may want to spend all day hidden in a corner, with no human contact. This would, perhaps, be a prime example of an irrational desire. But suppose this desire is based on the paranoid belief that people wish his death. The desire in this case would not be essentially irrational. The person's irrationality consists in having the

paranoid belief. Given the existence of the (irrational) belief, the
desire to avoid people may be itself quite rational. The irrationality
of having the paranoid belief is not compounded by coming to
have the desire. Humeans can readily accept desires which are
'irrational' in this sense, although they could claim, rightly, that,
strictly-speaking, it is not the desire which is irrational, but the
precipitating belief.

It is important to remember that the dispute is over whether or
not desires can be simply irrational without being dependent on
any faulty beliefs. As with many issues in moral and political
philosophy the dispute over whether or not there can be essentially
irrational desires is one which cannot be settled by formal proof.
A prime candidate for an essentially irrational desire is the urge
some people feel at the edge of a precipice, to leap off (see Parfit,
1984, p.122). For most people (excluding would-be suicides and
those who are attracted by the thought of soaring through the
air), there is no reason to leap off, and any desire to do so
appears to be an irrational impulse which should be resisted.

Whilst accepting that it would certainly be irrational for
someone to jump just because they had the urge, I do not think
this is an example of an essentially irrational desire. To explain
why it isn't, it is helpful to introduce some non-Humean
distinctions.

Actions result from beliefs about the nature and consequences
of possible courses of conduct combined with dispositions to
pursue certain goals. Let us call these dispositions 'inclinations'.
Usually a person is inclined to pursue a certain goal because she
believes there is something good or worthwhile about it. Let us
call these inclinations '*r*-desires' (to signify that they are backed
by reasons).

It may be possible to have an *r*-desire for something which is in
no respect worth desiring. However, this is not an essentially
irrational desire; for, by definition, a person *r*-desires something
because he believes it is, in some respect, worth desiring. If the
object of the *r*-desire turns out to be in no respect worth desiring,
the irrationality of *r*-desiring it, is the familiar kind – having a
desire based on an irrational belief. An example might be
someone's desire to possess an aphrodisiac, which turns out to be
completely ineffective. *R*-desires cannot be *essentially* irrational.

Not all inclinations are, however, backed by beliefs that their objects have anything good about them. The desire to leap off the precipice may be a case in point. Let us call inclinations to pursue a goal, in the absence of any belief that the goal is in any respect worth desiring, '*a*-desires' (to signify the absence of a supporting reason). Are *a*-desires essentially irrational?

People are inclined to say that it is irrational to *a*-desire to leap (to one's death) off a precipice. Whilst accepting that it would be irrational to act on such an *a*-desire, I think the Humean would be right to insist that there is nothing irrational about *having a*-desires. Consideration of a case where there are clear reasons against acting on an *a*-desire confuses the issue.

Let us consider an *a*-desire to stretch. Someone might just feel like stretching – not for any reason – not because of a belief that stretching would be worthwhile. If there is no reason not to stretch, then it would not be irrational to act on the urge. Here it is, perhaps, easier to see that the desire is just a feeling which, as it were, happens to one. It is neither rational or irrational to have this feeling, just as it is neither rational nor irrational to feel sick. *A*-desires may, like waves of nausea, just come and go. When beliefs and decisions to act are stripped away from inclinations, there is nothing left about the inclination to be irrational.

Desires, reasons and action

What about the Humean view of the connection between desires and reasons for action? Do all desires provides some reason for action, strength of reason being fixed by strength of desire? If there were essentially irrational desires, it would be reasonable to claim that they provide no direct reason for action. I have denied that such desires exist. However, I do think there is a good reason for rejecting the Humean view of the relation between desires and rational action.

As *a*-desires are inclinations to pursue a goal, in the absence of the belief that there is anything at all desirable in the goal, it is clear that the existence of an *a*-desire provides no *direct* reason for action. It does not follow from this that it is irrational either to have, or to act on *a*-desires. In a famous story, a donkey, now known as Buridan's Ass, was placed an equal distance between two similar buckets of hay. Because the donkey could not choose between the buckets, he remained rooted to the spot – and starved to death. It would not have been irrational for Buridan's Ass both to have and act on an a-desire to eat the hay in the left hand rather than the right hand bucket of hay.

It is, however, irrational to act on a mere a-desire (in the absence of indirect reasons to do so) whenever there is some reason not to. But what determines whether there is such a reason? What are the criteria of desirability, which in the end, fix what people have most reason to do? The Humean view of this is that 'the ultimate ends of human action can never . . . be accounted for by reason.' If there are no essentially irrational desires, perhaps this part of the Humean theory is salvageable. In contrast with the Kantian view, according to which the only ultimately desirable ends of human action are those justified by considerations of pure rationality, Hume is claiming that a person's ultimate ends, which generate her reasons for action, themselves cannot be divorced from her own personal non-rational 'affections'. Someone who doesn't care about the suffering of a stranger has no direct reason to help relieve his distress.

If desires never conflicted, then rational action would simply consist in pursuing whatever desires one had as efficiently as possible. However, they do conflict. How should such conflicts be resolved?

The Humean view does not offer a satisfactory solution to this problem. According to it, the rational thing to do is simply to act in pursuit of the strongest consistent set of desires one has. R-desires in themselves count for no more than a-desires, and r-desires of a given strength, supported by only weak reasons count for no less than equally powerful r-desires supported by strong reasons. This view underestimates the role of a deliberating agent in evaluating rival courses of action. Being creatures with a will, we are able to stand back from, disavow, and even counteract particular inclinations, even very strong inclinations. Such conduct may be a requirement of rationality, and therefore of autonomy.

Conclusion

The Humean view is appealing to those who anyway are inclined to believe that people should be left alone, as far as possible, to run their own lives; for it is a minimalist conception of autonomy. To be autonomous is simply to do as one chooses, provided one is not acting irrationally – and irrationality is avoided so long as one does not, in deliberation, use faulty reasoning.

I have argued that this view is right in its insistence that inclinations, when separated from accompanying beliefs and decisions to act, are non-rational occurrences, and that what a person has reason to do is not independent of his particular desires. However, the theory is defective as an account of rational deliberation about what to do. It suggests that the process of rational decision making is aimed simply at the production of *beliefs* which will enable one to act so as to satisfy the highest aggregate of current inclinations, strength of inclination being equivalent to strength of reason. It gives insufficient weight to the role of the agent as a deliberator, who can stand back from pushes and pulls, and decide how much weight to give to his various inclinations.

Whereas the *Kantian* is right to claim that rational agency, and autonomy, require the ability to act contrary to, even powerful inclinations, the *Humean* is right to assert that ultimate goals, which ground structured reasons, are themselves determined by non-rational inclinations (*a*-desires). An interesting consequence of this view is that any supposedly ultimate value faces a dual challenge: either it may not be ultimate (it is held for some further reason), or it may be defeated by other reason-based values. A rational Humean will be aware of the possibility that a supposedly ultimate value may enjoin conduct which is worse than an alternative: in which case the value should not be acted upon, since the value is valued for no reason at all. So although our so-called fundamental values provide reasons for acting on them, their own foundation remains insecure, and always, in principle, subject to destruction.

4 Socrates and the Fool

'no intelligent human being would consent to be a fool, no instructed person would be an ignoramus, no person of feeling and conscience would be selfish and base, even though they should be persuaded that the fool, the dunce, or the rascal is better satisfied with his lot than they are with theirs.' (Mill, 1861)

In the preceeding chapter I argued that the Humean view has two major shortcomings. First, its account of the relation between inclinations and reasons for action is false. Reasons for action are not directly proportional to strength of inclination. Second, the Humean account allows an insufficient role for the rational agent in action. Kant recognised the importance of active agency for autonomy, but his account of activity is flawed for reasons given in Chapter 2. In this chapter we shall discuss a view which, in many respects, combines what is best in the Humean view with a more adequate account of rational agency. The view is derived from the celebrated English liberal John Stuart Mill. Mill's famous essay *On Liberty* is one of the most powerful defences of the value of individual autonomy, even though 'autonomy' was not a term favoured by its author.

Brave New World

Aldous Huxley's novel *Brave New World* is about a well-structured society of contented people. Nearly all the citizens of Brave New World are satisfied with their lives; there is little strife or suffering of any kind within the society. And yet Huxley wrote his novel not to provide a blueprint for an ideal society, but as a warning. The Brave New World of his novel was a frightening picture of what might befall western societies, if passive consumerism is not held in check. Huxley wrote of this world in the foreword to the 1946 edition of his novel: 'It is quite possible that the horror may be upon us within a single century' (p.14).

The unifying principle of the different versions of utilitarianism is that the fundamental unit of comparison between different states of affairs is happiness. In other words, if happiness is better realised by state of affairs A than it is by state of affairs B, A is preferable to B. Were he to remain true to his version of utilitarianism, Jeremy Bentham (1748–1832), widely recognised as the founder of modern utilitarianism, would have to concede that Brave New World would be a big improvement on any known modern society, since the balance in that society, of pleasure over pain, was very pronounced. Many regard this as a *reductio ad absurdum* of Benthamite utilitarianism. Mill, on the other hand, could consistently share the common view that the world Huxley describes is far worse than contemporary society. A Millian could say that although the citizens of Brave New World were content, they were not happy, since for Mill autonomy is a vital constituent of happiness, and the citizens of Brave New World were, for the most part, denied the possibility of individual autonomy.

One shortcoming of the Humean view of autonomy is that, by its standards, there is no reason to call into question the autonomy or rationality of the citizens of Huxley's society. For they do as they choose – they are not forced to act against their will. And their conduct is successfully motivated by the pursuit of their desire-given ends. Their conduct is not guided by irrational beliefs about the consequences of their actions. When they anticipate anxiety they resort to the drug *soma*, which enables them to 'take a holiday from reality . . . without so much as a headache or a mythology'. They act, in Hume's sense, 'according to the determinations of the will'; that is, in accordance with their own settled preferences, not subject to the compulsion of others. Yet someone could call them autonomous only as a joke. So wherein lies their heteronomy?

The citizens are conceived in test tubes, gestated in laboratories, 'decanted' after nine months, and all except the top two of the five classes in the hierarchy are mass-produced to have ninety-odd identical siblings; so in a crucial sense they lack individuality.

During infancy and early childhood they are conditioned by a variety of techniques, including aversive behaviour modification, and 'hypnopaedic sleep teaching', during which they come to accept the *mores* of their class, and to be content with society and their place in it. It is not, however, because they are conceived in laboratories, the products of genetic engineering, that the people (especially Gammas, Deltas and Epsilons – the lowest three classes in the hierarchy) lack autonomy. For genetic engineering *per se* undermines autonomy no more than does the genetic lottery which produces people in our society. Furthermore, their heteronomy is not simply the result of their being subject to non-rational means of value-inculcation as infants and young children; for even in a less planned society children acquire basic values before the capacity for critical rationality, without thereby threatening subsequent autonomy.

The *origin* of people's personalities, values and capabilities may be relevant to the question of ultimate moral responsibility, but is not *directly* relevant to whether or not the people are, after these dispositions have developed, autonomous. There is no objection in principle, to using a programme of genetic engineering to increase people's autonomy (for a very helpful discussion of genetic engineering and autonomy see Glover, 1984). The most striking way in which the inhabitants of Brave New World are heteronomous on a Millian account is that they lack active theoretical rationality.

Theoretical rationality

It is theoretically irrational to make invalid deductive inferences, or use unsound induction, as when someone tries to establish a general law by simple enumeration of a few cases. I call the disposition to make only sound inferences 'passive theoretical rationality', because the disposition to accept only certain inference principles is not within one's direct control. It may be possible for people to bring it about that evidence before them is rejected. Moreover, someone could take a drug with the aim of acquiring false beliefs. But, where a belief is sustained through such non-truth-centred motives, awareness of this fact threatens the existence of the irrational belief.

Although passive theoretical rationality is essential to autonomy, there is an important part of theoretical rationality which may be more within the control of an agent. Full theoretical rationality requires a disposition to seek the truth, to ensure that one's beliefs are not false. This requires precisely the enquiring spirit which is so noticeably lacking among the citizens of Brave New World. It was not that they were especially prone to making invalid deductions and bad inductions; they simply had little interest in the truth. Their active theoretical rationality was severely limited.

Although I speak of active theoretical rationality, it is not clear that to have incomplete active theoretical rationality is in itself irrational. Although it is irrational to be overconfident that a belief one has is true, it is not necessarily irrational to rest content with less-than-certain beliefs, for which one lacks hard evidence. This is because information-seeking can be costly. On the other hand, in order to believe anything at all it is necessary to have *some* active theoretical rationality; for, as Bernard Williams (1970) put it, 'beliefs aim at truth'.

On the Humean account, the extent to which it is desirable for a person to be actively theoretically rational is fixed by her ultimate ends, such ends possibly varying from person to person with no implications of irrationality for anyone. Of course a person should have a *greater* interest in discovering the truth of some propositions rather than others; for their truth may be more significant for her. Someone proposing a transatlantic boat trip should, (unless he doesn't care whether he drowns) have very good evidence that the craft is seaworthy, whereas it is all right to rely on much less evidence before launching a model yacht on the village pond. If the citizens of Brave New World do not place a high premium on the truth of their opinions about the kind of society in which they live, there is nothing wrong (on Humean grounds) with not bothering to investigate critically the assumptions on which their lives and society are based; unless a failure to do this threatens the successful pursuit of their goals, in the sheltered world they inhabit.

In contrast with this instrumentalist account, Mill believed that active theoretical rationality was intrinsically desirable, apart from any instrumental value it may have. The Millian, unlike a Humean, regards a passion for truth as good in itself, as a constituent element of autonomy.

In Chapter 2 of *On Liberty* Mill mounts a vigorous defence of freedom of expression, arguing that it should be possible to hold and defend in public, without penalty, any opinions, no matter how absurd or pernicious they may seem at the time to the majority, or to the experts of the day. Some of his arguments appeal to the fact that limiting freedom of discussion may lead simply to the suppression of truth; for history is littered with examples of beliefs once held with the utmost conviction, which have subsequently shown to be false. But his most distinctive arguments appeal directly to autonomy, and to the intrinsic worth of active theoretical rationality. For example he writes the following about societies where there are strong disincentives for people to express heretical views:

> 'Those in whose eyes this reticence on the part of heretics is no evil should consider, in the first place, that in consequence of it there is never any fair and thorough discussion of heretical opinions; and that such of them as could not stand such a discussion, though they may be prevented from spreading, do not disappear. But it is not the minds of heretics that are deteriorated most by the ban placed on all enquiry which does not end in the orthodox conclusions. The greatest harm done is to those who are not heretics, and whose whole mental development is cramped, and their reason cowed, by the fear of heresy.' (Mill, 1859, p.94).

Although autonomy does not require the total obsession with theoretical rationality required by the Cartesian quest for the certain foundation for all beliefs, it includes a disposition to question received wisdom, or indeed any proposition one is inclined to accept; not just because this is a sound policy for realising one's goals, but out of concern for truth itself. It is clear why such a disposition is a requirement of pure rationality, but why should *it* be a requirement of autonomy, when the pure rationality of Kantian neutrality fails to be?

Truth

If a belief, desire, feeling or action is irrational, its possessor is open to criticism. For example, an irrational belief is one which, given the evidence available, the believer *should* not have. To be susceptible to irrational beliefs is one way in which a person's autonomy may be impaired. But irrationality is not the only kind of fault a belief may have, for there is a gap between rationality and truth. The possession of false, though not irrational beliefs may impose a serious limitation on the kind of control of one's own life, which autonomy requires.

One of the most insidious tools of tyranny is manipulation of the information which people must use in their deliberations. There is strong evidence that over the last 30 years military leaders in both the Soviet Union and the United States have produced misleading, or downright false information about the relative strengths of, and levels of expenditure on arms, in the two countries. It is not irrational, on the basis of information supplied, for citizens of the States to fear an attack from the Soviet Union, whether or not such an attack is actually likely. Othello was arguably not irrational to believe Iago. However, his killing of Desdemona was less than fully autonomous, because Othello would not have killed her were he not misguided by the false belief that she had been unfaithful.

Information is often manipulated in more subtle ways than through out-and-out lies. First, released information may be significantly selective. In public statements it is alleged, for instance, that the Soviet Union has more missiles than the United States, and should therefore reduce its weaponry to restore parity. This may be true, but it overlooks the crucial fact that missiles have different capabilities, and carry different numbers of warheads.

Another way in which information is manipulated is through stereotyping. Many school reading books have been criticised for their sexism, racism and nationalism. It is not that they *state* that girls are less adventurous than boys; but it is always Peter who climbs the tree, whilst Jane looks on. It is not that they *say* black people are stupid; but Epominandas, who is a stupid child, happens to be black. Advertisements frequently do not aim just to persuade people that their product is worth buying, but to sell a way of life. In a soap powder commercial a 'normal' family is portrayed – a wife who stays at home, and is especially concerned that her children's and husband's clothes be not just clean, but sparkling white. Her son plays rough and tumble games, and enjoys being covered in mud, whereas the only tumble which appears to interest the daughter (and there usually are two children – of opposite sexes) is the tumble dryer. The husband, when he comes home from work, plays with the children, whilst his wife prepares and brings him his food. Such a life is not only represented as available to those who use the particular product, but is presented in such a way that any alternative style of life is by implication deviant. Thus people's preferences come to be shaped by their, very often mistaken, views about what is *normal*, (in the non-statistical sense) and what alternatives are *feasible*.

Autonomy requires not just that people rationally pursue their not-irrational goals as best they can, but that they actually not be deluded about the nature of their goals, and the consequences of their actions. The extent to which someone is autonomous may then, be determined by external as well as internal cognitive failings. These external impediments to autonomy may be the result of the actions of others, or simply due to bad luck.

How does this connect with active theoretical rationality? Even rationally held straightforward factual beliefs may turn out to be false, so there can be no cast-iron guarantee that even *they* are true. With more controversial beliefs, in particular those religious, moral and political beliefs, which Mill calls 'opinions', the problem of error is especially acute. For here, not only are the very concepts subjects of dispute, but those in positions of power have strong other-than-truth-centred motives for promoting conformity – for example in beliefs about acceptable life styles, and feasible alternatives.

There is thus a danger that people will adopt life styles not because they represent truly their best options, but because they have not properly considered alternatives, and are carried along by the force of public opinion, or at least the opinions of influential individuals or groups.

Although there can be no guarantee of truth, the best defence against error is to have a commitment to active theoretical rationality for its own sake – especially in the controversial area of 'matters of opinion'. This requires that one not only have good reasons for one's own opinion, but also give proper consideration to rival opinions. In matters of opinion, an autonomous person should be in a position to refute opposing views. Mill writes of the person who maintains an opinion without considering reasons against it:

> 'he is either led by authority, or adopts, like the generality of the world, the side to which he feels most inclination . . . He must know them [the opposing views] in their most plausible and persuasive form; he must feel the whole force of the difficulty which the true view of the subject has to encounter and dispose of; else he will never really possess himself of the portion of truth which meets and removes that difficulty.' (Ibid., p.97)

The person who fails to consider properly alternative opinions to his own is either led by authority, in which case the principles to which he appeals for guidance in choosing a way of life, are *external* to him, or they are simply principles given by inclination – those he just feels attracted to – for no reason. In either case, although there may be no errors of reasoning, there is a lack of self-determination. This has the initially surprising consequence that most of us are not autonomous in regard to most of our scientific beliefs, and indeed that complete autonomy is unattainable for beings with finite minds. This is not as strange as it sounds, however, once it is remembered that autonomy is relative – to particular beliefs, desires and actions, and a matter of degree (people are more or less autonomous). Autonomy in regard to a particular set of beliefs, desires or actions does require an agent's relevant beliefs to be true, and that she be able to give a justification of them. However, autonomy, about, say, theoretical scientific beliefs, may be unimportant for most of us, since such beliefs are unlikely to have wide ramifications throughout our life projects. Hence a high level of active theoretical rationality regarding such matters is inessential.

The situation is quite different with so-called 'matters of opinion', for two reasons. First, given the intentional and unintentional pressures for social conformity, unless a person has a well-developed active theoretical rationality about 'opinions', it is likely that he will base important life decisions on false beliefs. Thus the initial heteronomy can ramify, with harmful consequences. Second, basic moral intuitions (opinions) are formed in early childhood at a time before the child has become a rational deliberator. The values expressed in these opinions are the values of other people, whether parents or significant others. Because a person's values, in their nature, ramify throughout their life, critical assessment of one's values (a significant part of active theoretical rationality) is especially important for most people's autonomy.

Whereas Kant believed that autonomy requires a person to become free of susceptibility to inclinations, Mill claimed that autonomy requires instead that a person's inclinations be genuinely his own:

> 'The same strong susceptibilities, which make the personal impulses vivid and powerful, are also the source from whence are generated the most passionate love of virtue, and the sternest self-control . . . A person whose desires and impulses are his own – are the expression of his own nature, as it has been developed and modified by his own culture – is said to have a character. One whose desires and impulses are not his own, has no character, no more than a steam-engine has a character. If, in addition to being his own, his impulses are strong, and under the government of a strong will, he has an energetic character.' (Ibid., p.118)

It is worth noting that Mill does not hold the view that characters can be formed by abstract individuals, completely uninfluenced by a culture. The claim is that people have their own distinct nature, which is shaped by culture, and this is consistent with the view that it would be impossible for a human being to develop a character except within a culture. Autonomy requires a person to reflect on the influences of her culture, to sort out those of her felt impulses which are really expressions of her unique nature, from those which are *merely* the product of external influences.

Self-determination and self-realisation

Kant believed that autonomy is so valuable because he thought it synonymous with the freedom from natural causation which is a prerequisite of genuine moral responsibility. We have already had a glimpse of the difficulties Kant encountered through supposing that human beings can govern their conduct by principles which are independent of natural causation. Although people are more or less autonomous, there is no coherent account of 'self-determinism', the view that uncaused selves can exert causal influence on the world through their actions. If, as I believe, self-determinism is a requirement of full-fledged moral responsibility, then to the extent that autonomy is possible, it cannot be identified with moral responsibility.

The allure of autonomy must lie elsewhere. To speak of reality is to draw an implicit contrast with (mere) appearance. Thus it may *appear* that the sun goes round the earth, but *in reality* the earth orbits the sun. By extension of the same principle it is possible to distinguish what a person really needs, from what he may appear to need. Someone who is cold may appear to need to put on a warm coat; but if she is suffering from hypothermia, wearing a coat might kill her. What she really needs is to be in a warm room with only light clothing, so that the warmth can get through to her quickly. To pursue merely apparent needs at the expense of real needs is to lack self-determination.

A need is a necessary condition. Thus we may speak not only of the needs of people, but also of the needs of cauliflowers, cows, cars and countries. It is clear from this that all needs are needs *for* something. The car needs petrol if it is to be able to run, whereas the cauliflower needs water and nutrients if it is to grow. The necessary conditions which we identify as needs are those which are essential for the *creature* in question to *flourish* if it is a living entity, or to *function* as it is intended if it is an *artefact*.

People share with plants and animals basic biological needs, such as those for food, drink, and protection from the elements and predators, which we may call 'security' needs. Many thinkers (see for instance Abraham Maslow, 1970) have supposed that human beings have higher level psychological needs, although attempts to produce and justify lists of such 'needs' have not been an unqualified success.

Among candidate 'needs' for human beings, are those to identify closely with one's fellow human beings, to identify with a national entity, to be artistically creative, to work, to have a family, to serve a group, to worship God, to be well-thought-of by others, and to have high self-esteem. Those who believe that human nature is such that one of these is a universal human need, have an at least in principle justification for trying to secure, by coercion if necessary, agreement on the necessity for the favoured goal. For this, and other reasons, it is with some scepticism that many political theorists regard claims about universal human needs. Such claims may be a thinly-veiled excuse for imposing the unpopular views of one section of society on another.

Mill also believed that there are human needs which transcend the purely biological needs for survival, physical pleasure, and the avoidance of pain. Yet his view is significantly different from those who believe that there is some *one* kind of pursuit which all human beings must engage in if they are to flourish. How could he adhere to both? The key lies in Mill's view of people as essentially creatures with a will, creatures with the ability to deliberate, and through deliberation, change their inclinations. The effects of deliberation on desires will vary from person to person according to their inherited constitution and the effects of their environment, notably cultural environment. The fact that we do have the capacity to deliberate gives us the chance of shaping our own lives, of developing what Mill calls a 'character'. Although it is his view that everyone has a need to realise their own particular character, he firmly rejects the view that there is a particular character type which everybody should develop. To the contrary he writes:

'Human beings are not like sheep; and even sheep are not indistinguishably alike. A man cannot get a coat or a pair of boots to fit him unless they are either made to his measure, or he has a whole warehouseful to choose from: and is it easier to fit him with a life than with a coat, or are human beings more like one another in their whole physical and spiritual conformation than in the shape of their feet? . . . Such are the differences among human beings in their sources of pleasure, their susceptibilities of pain, and the operation on them of different physical and moral agencies, that unless there is a corresponding diversity in their modes of life, they neither obtain their fair share of happiness, nor grow up to the mental, moral and aesthetic stature of which their nature is capable.' (Ibid., p.125)

Self-determination is in part a process of discovery, of finding out one's own capacities, and the limits to them. As there are no defined limits, and because such limits as there are may themselves be changed through reflection on what we do and think, this process is itself indeterminate and endless. The point is well put by John Gray (1983) in his excellent study of Mill's writings on liberty, to which I am indebted. He writes:

> 'According to this theory [Mill's theory of human nature], human beings are understood to be engaged in recurrently revising the forms of life and modes of experience which they have inherited, and by which 'human nature' itself is constituted in any given time and place. In this account of man as a creature engaged in an endless process of self-transformation, what distinguishes human beings from members of other animal species is only their powers of reflexive thought and deliberate choice.' (Gray, 1983, p.85)

We each have a unique, though changeable nature, which sets limits on what will enable us to flourish. So, for us to flourish, it is necessary to sustain this endless quest of self-evaluation and discovery. If self-determination is in part a process of discovery, the question arises of how one is to engage in this process? Mill plausibly claims that it is only through the unimpeded exercise of rational choice that such discovery is possible. Hence the need for active theoretical rationality and the other constituent elements of autonomy as an essential condition for self-realisation.

Mill's theory considered

The Millian view avoids each of the main weaknesses of the two other views so far considered. The Humean view gives insufficient weight to the *activity* of reflecting on what to do or believe, since according to it, people at best just follow their predominant inclinations. The Kantian account puts activity at the centre of autonomy, but misconceives the role of reason and inclination in rational decision making. The Millian account acknowledges that having and acting on strong inclinations is not inconsistent with autonomy. Indeed it recognises that autonomy requires an agent to take full account of the peculiarities of his own situation, and in particular of his own unique nature. Unlike the Humean view, however, it gives a cogent account of the activity of an autonomous deliberator. An autonomous agent does not just act on existing desires and beliefs, but subjects the desires and beliefs to rational scrutiny.

The major difficulty with a theory such as Mill's is in its dual claims about human nature – that we have a need for self-determination, and that, beyond this property, which gives us the same *formal* end, there is no single *substantive* end for humanity, it being of the nature of human nature that each individual human being has her own qualitatively unique essence.

The problem is that both claims are neither self-evident, nor readily testable empirically. To take the first: History is full of examples of people who have apparently been content to accept not only the received views of their society, but have no objection to being in a position of servitude. They have demanded neither education, nor the chance to experiment with novel lifestyles, nor participation in political systems. Even the majority of people in modern liberal democracies do not demand the opportunities to develop significantly their powers of self-determination.

Mill was certainly aware of these truths, and yet he believed that human beings could flourish only through being actively self-determining. In a famous statement in his essay *Utilitarianism* Mill wrote:

'It is better to be a human being dissatisfied than a pig satisfied; better to be Socrates dissatisfied than a fool satisfied. And if the fool, or the pig, are of a different opinion, it is because they only know their own side of the question. The other party to the comparison knows both sides.' (Mill, 1861, p.9)

Whilst human beings have never, we may assume, experienced what it is like to be pigs, they are able to represent the alternatives of being a pig or a human being to themselves, and would (almost all) choose to be human beings, even dissatisfied ones. On the other hand pigs, we may assume, lack the capacity for choice, at least a choice of the complexity of the one under consideration. However, fools can choose, and many people, it would appear, do prefer pleasant, heteronomous existence to a more challenging life of self-determination.

Mill compounds the problem by going on to answer an objection to his view in a way which looks suspiciously like special pleading. He acknowledges that some may reject his view on the grounds that people often do start out with youthful enthusiasm for what he calls the 'higher' pleasures, but then 'sink into indolence and selfishness'. Does this not show that active self-determination is a need only for some – the Socrates's of this world, for instance? Mill answers as follows:

'I do not believe that those who undergo this very common change, voluntarily choose the lower description of pleasures in preference to the higher. . . . Capacity for the nobler feelings is in most natures a very tender plant, easily killed, not only by hostile influences, but by mere want of sustenance; and in the majority of young persons it speedily dies away if the occupations to which their position in life has devoted them, and the society into which it has thrown them, are not favourable to keeping that higher capacity in exercise.' (Ibid., pp.9–10)

This looks like the introduction of an *ad hoc* hypothesis to protect Mill's thesis from falsification. Why are 'higher' pleasures better than 'lower' pleasures? Because nobody would voluntarily choose the latter over the former. But there do seem to be counter-examples. Yes, but those who choose the lower pleasures aren't *voluntarily* choosing. But what reason is there to suppose that those who have opted for the so-called 'lower' pleasures have not voluntarily chosen this course? Evidence may be hard to come by, and it won't do to say that nobody would voluntarily choose the lower of two pleasures, because a life devoted to the (successful) pursuit of lower pleasures is worse than one devoted to the (only partially successful) pursuit of higher pleasures. For what is at issue here is whether or not the so-called 'higher' pleasures of an autonomous existence, really *are* better than so-called 'lower' pleasures.

However, Mill did intend his view that the 'higher' pleasures really are better than the 'lower' to be empirically testable. If people begin their conscious lives without being autonomous, then those who become autonomous will have knowledge by

experience of both autonomy and heteronomy. Mill is prepared
to concede the *theoretical* possibility that mere sensual pleasures
are of as high or higher a quality than those of rational self-
determination, but he thinks this view false. How, then, are
higher pleasures to be distinguished from the lower?

'On a question which is the best worth having of two pleasures,
or which of two modes of existence is the most grateful to the
feelings . . . the judgment of those who are qualified by
knowledge of both, or if they differ, that of the majority among
them, must be admitted as final.' (Ibid., p.10)

His verdict, and it is plausible, is that people who are autonomous
would not be prepared to trade their autonomy for even very
large gains in pleasant mental states. To test whether you value
autonomy to this extent, consider whether you would wish to
trade your present life for a permanent existence on Robert
Nozick's celebrated 'experience machine'.

'Suppose there were an experience machine that would give
you any experience you desired. Superduper neuropsychologists
could stimulate your brain so that you would think and feel you
were writing a great novel, or making a friend, or reading an
interesting book. All the time you would be floating in a tank,
with electrodes attached to your brain.' (Nozick, 1974, p.42)

The expectation of someone who believes that autonomy is a
human need, would be that the vast majority of those who
understood what it would be like to go permanently on the
experience machine, would refuse – they would prefer to remain
autonomous and somewhat dissatisfied, than to feel contented
and stimulated, whilst living a life of illusion. Mill proposes the
following test for isolating the 'pleasures' which define people's
vital interests, that is the necessary conditions for them to flourish:

'Of two pleasures, if there be one to which all or almost all who
have had experience of both, give a decided preference,
irrespective of any feeling of moral obligation to prefer it, that
is the more desirable pleasure. If one of the two is, by those
who are competently acquainted with both, placed so far above

the other that they prefer it, even though knowing it to be attended with a greater amount of discontent, and would not resign it for any quantity of the other pleasure which their nature is capable of, we are justified in ascribing to the preferred enjoyment a superiority in quality, so far outweighing quantity as to render it, in comparison, of small account.' (Mill, 1861, p.8)

This is a very important claim, as it can form the basis for a distinctive version of utilitarianism, which takes seriously the Kantian principle that respect should be shown for *people*. Whereas, for Benthamite utilitarianism the ultimate goal of society should be to bring about the greatest balance of pleasure over pain, with no direct regard to how the pleasures and pains are distributed between people, Mill's version includes a weighting system with a built-in egalitarian principle of respect for persons.

If it is true that some pleasures are incomparably better than others (and some pains are incomparably worse than others), then a top priority is to ensure that as many people as possible have these pleasures and avoid these pains. One standard objection to (Benthamite) utilitarianism is that nothing in it rules out the morality of very well-attended gladiatorial contests. For if the bloodthirsty crowd were large enough, then no matter how great the pain of the contestants, it could be outweighed by the sum of (the admittedly small) pleasures of the members of the huge crowd. On the Millian view, these contests would not be justifiable, because death in gladiatorial contest is *qualitatively* worse than any amount of deprivation of watching such contests.

I think Mill is right to propose that there are vital interests in the sense I have mentioned, and the principle that anyone's non-vital interests should be promoted only if this is not at the cost of anyone's vital interests, is appealing, especially to those who believe in the importance of respect for the individual. However, Mill's view that *autonomy* is a vital interest, even for those who do not appear to want it, remains contentious.

The claim that those who are autonomous would say that no amount of 'lower' pleasure would compensate them for their loss of autonomy has some force. However, even if it were true (which it probably is), this would not establish that becoming autonomous is a vital interest of everyone. Suppose there were a powerful drug which greatly altered its takers' powers of critical reflection, and effectively reduced them to the level of contented imbeciles. One effect of the drug is that it makes those who take it prefer their condition post-drug to their previous condition (no matter what that condition was). Suppose they even say that no amount of the pleasure of their former life would compensate them for loss of their post-drug state. If the choices of those who have experienced both kinds of existence were on their own sufficient to determine the relative quality of each, then one would be forced to conclude that the pleasures of life after taking the drug were higher than those of even the most autonomous existence before. Indeed it would be in everyone's vital interests to take the drug, even if all were reluctant to do so. I am sure that neither Mill nor just about anyone else would be happy to accept this conclusion.

The conclusion can be avoided by placing a restriction on the 'choice criterion' for distinguishing 'higher' from 'lower' pleasures (the view that the higher pleasure is the one which those who have experienced both would choose for themselves). The choice after taking the drug is less acceptable than that made before, because after a person has taken the drug, by hypothesis, his powers of judgment have deteriorated. In determining which pleasures are 'higher' for a given individual (and it must in principle be possible that different pleasures may be higher for different people), it is necessary to refer not just to the actual choices which the person makes (preferences he expresses), but to the choices he would make were his choice unencumbered by a failure to realise the nature and consequences of each choice.

If most people whose choices were unencumbered would prefer a less pleasant, but more autonomous life to a more pleasant but less autonomous existence, it would be reasonable tentatively to accept the hypothesis that of those whose choices are encumbered in the above way, most would (were they free of the encumbrances) prefer the life of autonomy. Although it is tempting to conclude from this that it is reasonable to suppose that autonomy is a vital interest of most people (including those who do not agree because they are unable to make a well-informed choice on the subject), such a conclusion is unwarranted. For becoming well-informed may affect not only the judgments a person makes, but may affect her character in other ways – and thus change what is and isn't in her interests. Mill's choice criterion does not provide a neutral ground from which the vital importance of autonomy can be established. The argument eventually hits the same problem as befell the Deliberative Theory in Chapter 3. It seems that we cannot establish that autonomy is a vital interest of everyone by reference to merely *hypothetical* choices. The claim remains an article of faith, although one which is plausible, and at least not inconsistent with available evidence. I shall return to (though not resolve) this question in Chapter 10.

As for the second claim about human nature – that each person has his own nature, to be discovered and in part created, by activity – a Millian could argue along the following lines. The world, or even one society at a particular time, is full of all sorts of different characters who gain fulfilment in a wide variety of ways. Some, for example, are extrovert, others introvert, some musical, others not, some gregarious, others more solitary . . . the list is endless. Among 'those who know' there is unlikely to be any convincing majority opinion as to whether it is better to read novels than to go to the theatre, or to play squash rather than go swimming, or to be married rather than single. If there is a widespread disagreement, either large numbers of 'qualified' people are wrong, or people's individual needs vary. The latter is arguably a more plausible hypothesis.

Conclusion

The Millian approach to autonomy has the virtue of combining the Kantian insistence on rational activity with the Humean recognition that the ultimate ends of human beings may be as diverse as their sentiments. It certainly offers the most plausible account of why autonomy might be something especially valuable.

Although I have argued that Mill is unable to demonstrate that autonomy is a vital interest of everyone, my counterargument does not establish that his belief is false. I suspect that because the concept of flourishing or happiness is itself inescapably controversial, there is no Archimedean point from which to judge whether autonomy really is a vital interest of everyone. However, Mill's view does lend enormous weight to the liberal case for toleration and the protection of civil liberties. Indeed I shall argue in Chapter 7 that it is difficult to make sense of liberal objections to paternalistic interference in the lives of individuals, unless one grants the Millian assumption that autonomy is a vital interest of human beings.

Having looked at three different conceptions of autonomy I am now in a position to propose a liberal conception of autonomy which will combine the strengths, whilst avoiding the drawbacks of these accounts. This will be the task of the next chapter.

5 A Liberal Conception of Autonomy

Conative heteronomy

The Millian account of autonomy is the most promising of those discussed so far. For it combines the Kantian insight that human beings are not just the passive victims of whatever passions happen to beset them with the Humean insight that the goals which it is rational for a given person to pursue are relative to his own distinct characteristics. The preferred conception which I shall put forward is not inconsistent with the Millian view, but adds to it.

I argued in Chapter 3 that the Humean view failed to give proper weight to the *activity* of a rational agent. This is partly because Hume did not address himself to the question of active theoretical rationality – regarding theoretical rationality rather just in its role as automatic producer of sound inductive and deductive judgments. Mill put that right by stressing the importance of an active desire for truth. The other respect in which Hume failed to give an adequate account of rational agency was in his reduction of all irrationality to the theoretical. Kant believed there was a distinctive realm of practical irrationality, concerning the activity of the will; but we have rejected Kant's own account of this. An adequate conception of autonomy requires a satisfactory concept of heteronomy *of the will*. For actions may go wrong either at the stage of deliberation, or after deliberation is complete.

Hume believed that there could never be a direct conflict between reason and passion, because his psychology was too simple. He believed that the only way in which a passion, desire or preference could be irrational is if it is founded on a false belief. Strictly-speaking, as we have argued, he should have said 'founded on an *irrational* belief'. No conflict could occur, according to him, because, as soon as a person realised that a passion was founded on a false belief, the passion disappeared, as it were, without offering any opposition:

> 'The moment we perceive the falsehood of any supposition, or the insufficiency of any means our passions yield to our reason without any opposition. I may desire any fruit as of an excellent relish; but whenever you convince me of my mistake, my longing ceases.' (Hume, 1739, pp.416–17)

This may well be true for fruit, but is not universally true of passions; and people continue to pursue goals which they realise are worthless, or lack the quality that initially made them desirable. To be autonomous requires an agent to pursue her desire-grounded goals, but this is not equivalent to acting on one's current strongest inclinations. An autonomous agent must not be the slave of her passions. Autonomy requires more of an agent than simply that he does as he chooses provided that his choice does not rest on irrational or false beliefs. There are two ways in which a person can suffer from what I shall call 'conative heteronomy' – i.e. from failure of the will properly to order inclination. I shall discuss each briefly.

Freedom of the will and levels of desire

As creatures with a will we are able to act in the light of deliberation about our beliefs and desires. Whereas a non-rational animal will act on whatever inclination is strongest at a particular time, human beings are able, at least sometimes, to defer immediate gratification, to choose that option which they think is best overall. This entails that we have desires, and therefore preferences, of different levels. Not only do we have desires, but we also have desires about our desires. In an influential paper Harry Frankfurt (1971) uses the distinction between different levels of desire to explicate what he calls 'freedom of the will'. I believe that to have a free will in Frankfurt's sense is a distinct necessary condition for autonomy. What, then, is 'freedom of the will' in Frankfurt's sense?

Consider the statement '*A* wants to *X*', where *X* refers to an action, *A* to an agent. Knowing simply that *A* wants to *X* is insufficient to determine whether or not *A* will try to do *X*, even if he has the chance. For example, *A* might realise that doing *X* is incompatible with doing *Y*, and he wants to *Y* more than he wants to *X*. Moreover, a person is not even always motivated by his current strongest individual desire – consideration of other desires may provide greater motivational force than the single strongest desire. This entails a distinction between 'want' or 'desire' (I use the two interchangeably), and what we may call an agent's 'will'. Frankfurt draws the distinction as follows:

> 'To identify an agent's will is either to identify the desire (or desires) by which he is motivated in some action he performs, or to identify the desire (or desires) by which he will or would be motivated when or if he acts.' (Frankfurt, 1971, p.8).

An agent's will, then, is the outcome of all motivational forces upon the agent, and directs her conduct. Where in a sentence of the form '*A* wants to *X*', *X* refers to an action, the want is a 'first-order' desire. But not all desires are of the first order. We have, in addition, wants about our wants. These are 'second-order' desires. There are two types of second-order desire. First, though this is surely a rarity, an agent might just want to find out what it would be like to have a particular first-order desire. Frankfurt gives the example of a doctor who wants to discover how it feels to have an addictive craving for a drug. He wants to want to take heroin, even though, of course, he does not want this desire to take heroin to become his will. He has no desire to form the intention to take heroin. This sort of second-order desire is not relevant to a conception of autonomy. The other kind, which Frankfurt calls 'second-order volitions', is crucial.

> 'Suppose a man wants to be motivated in what he does by the desire to concentrate on his work. It is necessarily true, if this supposition is correct, that he already wants to concentrate on his work. The desire is now among his desires. But the question of whether or not his second-order desire is fulfilled does not turn merely on whether the desire he wants is one of his desires. It turns on whether this desire is, as he wants it to be, his effective desire or will.' (Ibid., p.10)

Frankfurt claims that it is our possession of second-order volitions which morally marks off people from other creatures. It is because we have second-order volitions that it makes sense to talk of the possibility of free will. In order to have a free will in this sense, an agent must be able to make her will as she wants it to be. Such freedom is a necessary condition of autonomy.

The picture is like this. We all have desires, often conflicting desires, of various strengths. Because we have a will we are able to deliberate about our desires. Autonomy requires that our will is as we want it to be. In other words, the desires which actually motivate us should be the desires we want, after all deliberation has taken place, to motivate us. Someone of whom this is not true, is not in control of his own conduct.

Non-rational animals lack the possibility of autonomy because they simply act on their strongest (first-order) desires. They lack the capacity for higher-order desires. A person will inevitably experience conflict between some first-order desires and second-order desires. Sometimes a person will govern his conduct when there is such a conflict, in accordance with his second-order desires. Here is an example. You want another drink; but, because you don't want to run the risk of driving dangerously, you want that this want not become your will. You succeed in satisfying this second-order desire, and resist the temptation of another drink. Your will, in respect of whether or not to accept another drink, is free. Your decision to refuse is, to that extent, autonomous. Here is an example of *heteronomy* of this kind. A partially reformed heroin addict wants another fix. He also wants that this want not become his will. However, it does become his will – he heteronomously has another fix.

In principle there is no limit to the levels of desire it is possible to have. I may have a (third-order) desire that a certain second-order desire become my will. Autonomy requires that a person's will be in accordance with his highest-order preference. For simplicity, I shall, however, speak of the necessity for conduct to be governed by second-order desires.

It is a necessary condition of autonomy of the will that one's higher-order volitions are not dominated by first-order desires; for if one's will is not as one wants it to be, then it cannot be being determined by one's self. However, this is not sufficient.

Second-order volitions usually reflect a person's judgments

about what would be best, overall, to do. However, this is not necessarily the case: a thoroughly demoralised person, whilst recognising that a certain course of action would be for the best, may have ceased caring what happens to him. For example, an inveterate heroin addict may believe that the best thing for him to do is to abandon his habit; yet he has lost the second-order volition that he resist his first-order desire to have another fix. He indulges the first-order desire heteronomously. For a person's will to be autonomous, it must be as he wants it to be; but it must be in accordance with what he judges to be best.

Weakness of will

The failure to act in accordance with one's judgment about which of the considered alternatives would constitute the best action is often called 'weakness of will'.

Although I agreed with Hume that no substantive ends of conduct are requirements of rationality alone, this does not exclude the possibility of there being a formal goal of practical rationality. This goal may, loosely, be expressed as 'do as well as you can'. Autonomy requires of an agent that he not act irrationally; and rationality requires an agent to do as well as he can in his conduct. Yet people sometimes choose an option which is worse – even by the standards of their own personal preferences.

A common failure is irrationally to fail to give proper weight to evidence, say, that a particular action would be very risky, or that the long-term consequences of a particular strategy are likely to be harmful. Examples of this are easy to come by, and include some of those who still refuse to wear seat belts in cars, and some who continue to smoke cigarettes. It doesn't include all, for some smokers and seat-belt resisters are fully aware of the risks, and are quite prepared to take them – preferring, say, the immediate pleasure of nicotine intoxication and an increased change of pain and ill health in the future, to the immediate pain of nicotine deprivation with improved long-term chances.

When a person irrationally fails to consider evidence about the harmfulness of an action he intends to perform, the irrationality is usually caused by a desire, for instance, to continue to smoke. Although this irrationality is *caused* by a desire, and is a form of heteronomy, it is strictly speaking a failure of cognition – of theoretical, not practical rationality.

Weakness of will is easily confused with this sort of irrationality, but really is distinct. Weakness of will occurs when an agent, having considered two alternatives, arrives at the judgment that it would be better to perform one, and yet intentionally performs the other. There has been great controversy about weakness of will ever since Plato, and some regard it as strictly impossible on the grounds that a requirement of *intentional* action is that the agent judges that the chosen action is better than all considered options. I believe the phenomenon is possible, and is a not uncommon kind of heteronomy. It is, incidentally, worth noting that weakness of will does not always lead the weak-willed person to pursue selfish, rather than altruistic goals.

Weakness of will is well illustrated by this extract from Iris Murdoch's novel *The Bell*. The heroine, Dora, arrives at the station early, and finds a seat on the train. Soon the train fills up, until no empty seats remain. An elderly woman stops in the doorway of Dora's compartment. She is apparently a friend of the person sitting next to Dora, and it transpires that the two had hoped to travel together. Dora deliberates about whether to give up her seat to the elderly woman:

> 'She had taken the trouble to arrive early, and surely ought to be rewarded for this . . . There was an elementary justice in the first comers having the seats . . . The corridor was full of old ladies anyway, and no one seemed bothered by this, least of all the old ladies themselves; Dora hated pointless sacrifice. She was tired after her recent emotions and deserved a rest. Besides, it would never do to arrive at her destination exhausted . . . She decided not to give up her seat.
> She got up and said to the standing lady "Do sit down!"'
> (Quoted in Borger and Cioffi, 1970, p.229)

Being autonomous and exercising autonomy

To be an autonomous person is to possess certain intellectual and practical capabilities. However, it is possible to be autonomous in this sense, and yet have very little opportunity to exercise one's autonomy. A prisoner languishing in his cell may have a strong, well-ordered will, be a clear, active, rational thinker, under no illusions – and yet be able to do hardly anything. Is he more autonomous than someone who although less rational, is able to move freely about the world?

The question perhaps rests on a confusion between being autonomous and exercising autonomy. However, it is important for those who take seriously the value of promoting autonomy among people. In trying to produce a conception of autonomy, one is primarily interested in 'being autonomous', with the question 'what is it to be autonomous?' On the other hand, in discussing possible policies in regard to respect for people's autonomy, the question of the exercise of autonomy is central. For there may be conflicts between people's interests in the current exercise of autonomy, and in their interests in being autonomous later. Nevertheless, even here, our main attention will be on the importance of being autonomous, for if a person is not autonomous, the question does not even arise of his making or being denied the opportunity to make, autonomous choices.

To be perfectly autonomous is impossible for a finite intelligence. However, there may be a certain level of autonomy which it is necessary to reach, in order to be consistent with human dignity. Reaching this level would be far more important morally than attaining even higher levels of autonomy (see Chapter 7).

The conception

Autonomy is a matter of degree. Rather than trying to give a definition of what perfect, or complete autonomy would consist in, I think it is more helpful to set out the different ways in which a person may be heteronomous. Heteronomy is either cognitive (to do with belief), or conative (to do with the will). Just as we may loosely speak of someone being autonomous (if their beliefs, desires and actions are not too heteronomous), so we may loosely speak of someone being heteronomous (if they tend to have serious failings of autonomy). These descriptions are bound to be vague. In this respect autonomy is like baldness. We know what perfect baldness would consist in, but we use the word 'bald' to describe people who have lost a substantial amount of hair. It would be idle to attempt a precise definition of how many hairs, or what proportion of hair, a person must have lost in order to be correctly described as bald. It would be similarly idle to attempt a precise definition of just how heteronomous a person had to be to be properly called 'a heteronomous person'. Instead, I offer a conception which simply characterises ways of failing of autonomy, that is, being heteronomous. I believe it is an adequate liberal conception.

> An agent *A* is *cognitively* heteronomous with respect to a particular belief or set of beliefs if either *A* holds that belief or set of beliefs on account of a failure of *A*'s passive or active theoretical rationality, or the belief or set of beliefs is false.
>   *A* is *conatively* heteronomous with respect to a particular action or set of actions if either *A* acts through domination by lower-order desires, or *A* acts through weakness of will.

Conclusion

This view of autonomy combines the Kantian insight that the will is central to autonomy, with Hume's view that no substantive ends are required by rationality or autonomy alone, and Mill's insistence on the importance of critical, rational enquiry. In the rest of the book this is the conception I shall adopt. The intrinsic value of autonomy consists in the value of being relatively free of the forms of heteronomy mentioned above, and being able to put this capacity into practice.

This conception is liberal in that it allows considerable discretion to the individual agent over her or his choice of ends or lifestyle. I shall take it as axiomatic for liberal democracy that people's autonomy should be respected. But how should the principle of respect for autonomy be interpreted, and incorporated into political practice? These questions will occupy the next two chapters.

PART II

PRINCIPLES

One of the assumptions of this book is that autonomy, whatever it is, is something valued highly in liberal democratic societies. To identify and correctly characterise values is but one task of political theory. In this part of the book there will be a discussion of different ways of encapsulating the value of autonomy in political principles.

People may agree that autonomy is valuable, share a common conception of autonomy, and yet disagree about how autonomy should be promoted in society. My chief aim in this part is to discuss different principles in order to bring out some of the difficulties of trying to develop and justify plausible mechanisms for translating values into political practice.

6   Respect for Autonomy

Different attitudes towards values

Most people believe that lying is wrong. But there is by no means a consensus amongst such people about why lying is wrong, or about how one should go about promoting honesty. On the one hand are those who believe simply that, other things equal, it is better not to lie, because lying tends to produce harmful consequences. They don't think lying is *in itself* wrong. As things are rarely equal, lying is, on this view, often justifiable; for instance, in a medical context, to protect a patient from receiving information which might be painful. On the other hand, many people believe that lying is wrong in itself – independently of any other harms it may produce.

In general, valued objects or practices either have *intrinsic* worth (they are valued for their own sake), or merely *instrumental* worth (their value consists simply in promoting something else which has intrinsic worth). With this distinction in mind I shall write of intrinsic and instrumental values.

Intrinsic values are regarded in two ways: either they are thought to impose *moral constraints* upon their adherents, or they are regarded as *goals*. To illustrate the difference let us consider the statement 'Lying is wrong'. Among those who believe lying is intrinsically wrong, one finds two different attitudes towards lying. Some believe that it is always wrong to lie – even if telling a lie is the only way of preventing worse evils from occurring, for example that more lies are told overall. Those who hold this view regard the principle 'Do not lie' as a moral constraint upon action. Others, while believing that lying is intrinsically wrong, think that it may sometimes be right to lie – to prevent something worse than lying from occurring, or to prevent more lies being told. They regard the promotion of honesty as a goal.

Act utilitarians in the tradition of Bentham would regard autonomy as merely of instrumental value. According to them its value consists simply in being an effective means to the promotion of pleasure and the avoidance of pain. If there are any conflicts between the claims of autonomy and those of pleasure-and-the-avoidance-of-pain, a Benthamite would have to sacrifice the claims of autonomy. A Benthamite has no serious principled objection to life in Huxley's Brave New World, nor to a permanent existence on Robert Nozick's 'experience machine'. As long as the machine really *could* provide an exciting range of experiences, which on balance were pleasant (and not boring), a Benthamite would have to say that it would be best for most, if not all of us, to plug into this machine for life. The thought experiment of the experience machine is set up by Nozick as a *reductio ad absurdum* of Benthamite utilitarianism. The fact that few people would choose a life on the experience machine shows that we value things for their own sake, other than pleasant mental states. In particular autonomy is viewed as intrinsically valuable.

But if autonomy is intrinsically valuable, how should principles of respect for autonomy be regarded? I shall first consider a Kantian approach, which regards autonomy as imposing a moral constraint upon conduct.

Conflicts

One of the most attractive features of the Kantian treatment of autonomy, which it shares with Mill's, is the enormous weight given to respect for autonomy. Autonomy is so precious that we are asked by Kant to act in such a way that we *always* treat ourselves and each other never simply as means, but also as ends in ourselves. Using people for even laudable goals is strictly forbidden.

In fact in his political writings, as H. Williams (1983) argues, Kant maintained that it was not merely inevitable, but in some sense acceptable, for politicians to act other than virtuously, since they had to make public decisions in an imperfect world of flawed human beings. Nevertheless, the injunction of the categorical imperative *is* supposed to bind all rational creatures at all times –

whether in their public or private capacity – and I wish to
investigate what happens when one takes the *moral* theory at face
value.

It is wrong to secure political advantage through deception
because this fails to respect the autonomy of the deceived citizens.
The practical test for whether you are showing this respect is
whether the policy you are pursuing is one which the other party
could rationally endorse. I think the 'could' here should be
construed as meaning 'either does rationally endorse, or would
endorse if she or he considered the relevant facts of the case'
(leaving aside, though acknowledging, the difficulty of specifying
what is meant by 'considered the relevant facts'). As Kant himself
writes:

> 'the man who has a mind to make a false promise to others will
> see at once that he is intending to make use of another man
> *merely as a means* to an end he does not share. For the man
> whom I seek to use for my own purposes by such a promise
> cannot possibly agree with my way of behaving to him, and so
> cannot himself share the end of the action.' (Kant, 1785, p.92)

This may seem an overstatement. Why could not someone agree
that I acted correctly in deceiving them? To deceive someone is
to inculcate in him or her a belief which you take to be false. It is
true that nobody could, at a given time, knowingly acquire a
belief which he or she, at that time, takes to be false. In this
sense Kant is clearly right. However, someone may come to
believe later that the deception was justified, say because it was,
in the harsh political climate of the day, the only way of
preventing the people from suffering another five years of severe
oppression, including, perhaps, widespread deception by the
government.

It seems to me that what is essential to the Kantian view is its
requirement that people respect the wills of others. It is
illegitimate to treat the projects of other rational creatures with
less respect than you treat your own. Your policy has to be one
which the other endorses, or would endorse were you able to
explain it to him properly. This, I think, is at the heart of the
Kantian injunction about autonomy. The crucial question to ask a
potential victim of, say, deception is: 'How could I truthfully

explain my actions to this person, so as to make them rationally acceptable to her?'. This excludes the acceptability of securing agreement at the cost of deception, or any other form of non-rational manipulation.

One reason why the injunction: 'Never treat a human being simply as a means to an end' is problematic is that people exist through time, and it may be possible to satisfy the injunction at one time only by falling foul of it at another. To bring out the extent of the problem let us develop the above example.

Suppose you live in a country with a very authoritarian government and a very biased press, television and radio. This government has systematically, and possibly unsystematically, fed people misinformation. However, the form of democracy still exists, and elections are held. You believe that the election of your party will be better for the electorate, not least because it will better promote their autonomy. Unfortunately, on account of the effectiveness of the government's propaganda machine it is impossible to gain sufficient electoral support whilst remaining scrupulously honest about the reality of the austerity which will inevitably succeed the election. To have any chance of winning it is necessary to go some way to matching the extravagant claims of the government of the day. If you believe that people's autonomy should be respected – because it is wrong to treat people simply as means to ends – what should you do? What is the best way to regard the injunction?

If you think of respect for autonomy as imposing a *moral constraint*, as the categorical imperative seems to require, you should be scrupulously honest. At the time of the election campaign you will have respected the autonomy of the electorate. However, you might recognise that this policy would ruin your chances of election, and thus damage the long-term autonomy interests of the electorate.

On the other hand, if you adopt the *goal* of promoting the people's autonomy, you will certainly be treating them at the time of the election campaign, as means to an end (since you will deceive them), albeit an end which they will, one hopes, come to share.

A Kantian could argue here that you would not be treating them *merely* as a means to an end, since your policy is guided, at least in part, by the desire to promote ends which you perceive them to have at the time. A more general Kantian solution to this type of problem might be to drop the insistence that respect for autonomy requires one, at all times, never to engage in a policy which is motivated by a goal which the other party cannot share *at the time* one acts. After all, concern is for people throughout their lives, and if I treat someone as a means to the end of his own long-term autonomy, I am showing a more serious and sensible respect for his autonomy than I would be if I failed to manipulate him on one occasion to prevent far worse manipulations later. If I acted in the former way I would not be treating the *person* simply as a means to an end, since any present attack on her autonomy is more than compensated by her long-term gains, not least in autonomy.

Although this strategy offers a plausible solution to the *temporal* problem, the *interpersonal* problem is more intractable for the Kantian view. If people's autonomous goals really never conflicted, then it would be possible always to respect fully people's autonomy. People would share common goals if, as Kant suggests they should be, they were always motivated by strictly neutral principles; but in fact people's goals do sometimes conflict, and in these cases the prescription of the Kantian view may be not just ethically questionable, but literally impossible to execute.

To illustrate this let us return to the case of the authoritarian government. Suppose the government is several degrees worse than the one I described above. It is a blatantly fascist government, which has already begun a policy of genocide against an ethnic minority. Elections have been suspended, and all attempts peacefully to persuade the government to alter its policies have failed. The only feasible way to save the lives of the threatened minority is to stage an armed rebellion. One foreseen consequence of armed rebellion is that people are killed and wounded. How, in these circumstances might one follow the injunction: 'Never treat people simply as a means, but always at the same time as ends in themselves'?

Could one, consistent with the Kantian principle, justifiably kill soldiers loyal to the present rulers? If the mark of treating someone as an end in himself is that you act on a principle which the other finds acceptable, or would come to find acceptable if subject to rational persuasion, it is not clear that any principle which could plausibly justify killing the soldiers would, if enacted, treat them as ends in themselves. Their lives are being threatened as a means to the end of saving the lives of other people.

A strict Kantian could, I suppose, argue that the soldiers loyal to the tyrannical government were not acting autonomously in defending the tyrants, so that thwarting their will would not be a violation of their autonomy. Were they truly autonomous, and therefore purely rational, and therefore motivated by impartial principles, they would not support the tyrant. This at least is consistent with the plausible view that it is not wrong to prevent people from acting wrongly. However it is open to objections. First, as we have seen, the Kantian equation of autonomy with pure rationality is questionable. Second, very few people do act from pure Kantian motives, so interpreting the Kantian principle in this way would sanction such a widespread disregard of people's projects, as to make the principle almost vacuous in practice. Finally, although the soldiers' support of the tyrants might be heteronomous, one may suppose that others of their goals, which require them to stay alive, would not be. Therefore, by killing them, one would be violating their autonomy – for the sake of others – one would not be treating them as ends in themselves.

Another Kantian strategy might to be argue that the principle really applies only to those who accept it, as part of a mutually binding contract. My right to be treated by you as an end in myself depends on my recognition that you have a similar right to be so treated. The tyrants and their defenders forfeit their right to be treated in this way by the oppressed, because they fail to recognise the rights of others. This amendment may, however, be too great for a Kantian. It may exclude too many people from the category of those who are to be treated as ends in themselves. Young children, for example, do not typically accept the Kantian principle. Yet it would be an odd morality indeed which declared it all right to use children for whatever purposes would best serve adults, with no non-instrumental concern for the needs of the children.

To avoid this unwelcome consequence it could be argued that the tyrant and his supporters, unlike the child, deserve to be treated in this way because they know, or should know, better. Although this is a plausible move for those who accept the possibility of genuine moral responsibility, it marks a clear departure from the original Kantian injunction, which appeared to rest on the claim that respect is due to people in virtue of the fact that they have the *capacity* to act in pursuit of self-chosen goals, rather than on account of their actual moral virtue.

The difficulty does not, however, end here. For in any armed conflict it is inevitable that innocent people will suffer. If, for example, the war effort requires the destruction of a munitions dump, it is most likely that the bombing raid to destroy it will injure or kill some people who are not responsible for the tyranny. Those killed would probably include local inhabitants, who do not work at the factory, and do not support the government directly or indirectly. What is the rebel to say of these innocent victims?

Perhaps the most natural thing to say is that although it is awful that innocent lives should be lost, this is sadly the only way to avoid even greater loss of life and suffering, and is therefore justifiable. If there were any other way of overthrowing the tyrannical government, the rebels would pursue it. Nevertheless, in the circumstances described, the victims *are* forced to surrender their lives, quite independently of whether they agree with the rebels' principles. To deny that the innocent victims are being treated simply as a means to the end of the prevention of great suffering would, to say the least, be disingenuous. Admittedly they are not forced to give up their lives just to satisfy a whim; but the action undoubtedly destroys their chances of pursuing their own projects, and their will in regard to the action is irrelevant to whether or not it is going to happen.

To regard the principle of treating people as ends in themselves as a moral constraint upon action, leads directly to absolute pacifism, according to which it is always wrong to use violence against another, even if this is the only way of preventing even greater violence being perpetrated.

I believe that absolute pacifism is indefensible. To see whether you find it acceptable consider the case of James Huberty.

On 18 July 1984 James Huberty, armed with three guns, began what came to be known as the Macdonald's massacre. He entered a Macdonald's hamburger bar in San Diego, California, and declared that, having already killed a thousand people, he was going to kill a thousand more. He began shooting innocent people in the bar. Police and relatives were called to the scene to persuade Huberty to give himself up. All attempts failed. He killed twenty people, and all the indications were that he would carry on killing, unless and until he was forcibly stopped. The only way he could be prevented from killing more innocent people was for someone to shoot him. The massacre ended abruptly when a police marksman shot Huberty dead. Was it wrong to kill him? This action would certainly be ruled out by absolute pacifism. But suppose that, as a result of everyone on the scene with access to a gun being an absolute pacifist, Huberty had carried on his killing. What would they be able to say to his subsequent victims, or to their relatives? In what sense could they be said to have treated the victims as ends in themselves? It is most likely that the principles which led the onlookers to behave in this way would be unacceptable to the victims and their family and friends. The absolute pacifists would have been knowingly instrumental in the deaths and injuries, since they would have known that they could have behaved in a way which would have prevented them; but they chose to behave differently – for what? In order, perhaps, to avoid violating the Kantian principle in regard to the killer. But this looks remarkably like using the killers' victims as means to the end of one's own moral purity, which itself would be a violation of the principle in regard to the victims. This, of course, is not to deny that a morally sensitive person would, and arguably should, find it very difficult to use violence, even to prevent violence. The fact that someone was unable to pull the trigger might prevent him from acting rightly, but would by no means suggest he was a villain.

I know of two remaining avenues of escape for a defender of the Kantian view, but I suspect that each leads to a blind alley.

First, it could be argued that in the actual world we inhabit, with widespread conflicts of interest between people, there are occasions where it just *is* impossible to avoid acting wrongly. These have been called 'moral tragedies'. Bernard Williams (1965) and elsewhere, has argued that this phenomenon should be taken much more seriously by moral theorists. One feature of 'moral tragedies' is that no matter what you do, you are bound to feel (and should feel) morally awful, because you will have violated one of your firmly-held moral convictions.

R. M. Hare (1981) has pointed out that, whereas there may be situations in which no matter what a morally sensitive person does he is bound to feel morally awful, this does not entail that in them it is impossible to avoid wrong-doing. We acquire, for our everyday lives, sets of principles which guide our conduct, and the thought of transgressing which is morally painful. A person may find herself in the unfortunate position where it is impossible to satisfy the injunctions of at least one of the principles. The guilt we may feel is an inescapable by-product for most human beings, of adherence to the moral principles. As it is good, on the whole, that we adhere to these principles, the guilt we experience in 'moral tragedies' may be a price worth paying. In cases of serious conflict between the demands of one's regular action-guiding principles it is necessary to ascend to what Hare calls the level of 'critical thinking', in which one challenges the principles by reference to their underlying rationale. If there *were* a dispute-settling grand principle to which one could appeal, such as utilitarianism, there would at least be a procedure for deciding what to do, even if each of the possibilities is in a sense morally unthinkable.

The worst problem for the Kantian principle is that the conflict is present within a single principle. In a world where vital interests conflict it is just impossible to treat everyone as ends in themselves. If it is wrong to treat anyone as other than an end in him or herself, then in the sort of difficult case we are considering, it is impossible to avoid wrongdoing. Yet in such situations one needs to make a decision, and the view that as you are damned anyway, it doesn't matter what you do, would be too much a counsel of despair to appeal to anyone other than perhaps, a *very* romantic existentialist. On the other hand, to choose the lesser of two evils (or wrongdoings) as such, is substantially to reject the 'moral constraint' view.

The remaining strategy for the Kantian is to appeal to principles which would rule out the possibility of moral tragedy, even in a world of genuine conflicts of vital interest. There is, first, the acts/omissions doctrine, according to which, although it is wrong to harm someone through deliberate action, it may not be to do so through deliberate failure to act. In the case of the callous gunman, if you fail to shoot him, it is true that among the causes of the innocent people's being shot is your failure to shoot the gunman. However, your omission is condonable, for you haven't *done* anything to his victims. On the other hand, to shoot the gunman would be to do something to him which is inconsistent with the respect required by the Kantian principle.

A second principle is the so-called doctrine of 'the double effect', according to which there is a big moral difference between harm which is the result of what you strictly intend in your conduct, and harm which is merely a foreseen, though unintended consequence. If I shoot the gunman I might be said strictly to intend his death, whereas if I fail to prevent the murder of the innocents this is merely a foreseen consequence of my failure to shoot the gunman; it is not strictly intended.

There has been much discussion of these two principles in recent years, and both principles have been shown to be difficult to defend. Of the former, once it is clear wherein lies the difference between deliberate actions and deliberate failures to act, it emerges that the difference is insufficient to ground a moral distinction which has to carry the weight its defenders ask it to bear. Of the second principle, one can argue that there are no adequate criteria for distinguishing what is strictly intended in an action from what, although not strictly intended, is foreseen by the agent. I am persuaded by the criticisms which have been brought against the two doctrines, and rather than repeat the specific criticisms here, I shall refer you to two of the most lucid and persuasive criticisms, in Glover (1977, Chapter 7) and Bennett (1981).

For these reasons I reject a Kantian account of how the value of autonomy should be realised. I do not believe that the non-violation of people's autonomy should be regarded as an exceptionless moral constraint on action. It is possible, and in the real world, likely, that concern for autonomy will justify the violation of some people's autonomy some of the time, not least in the cause of respect for autonomy itself. The promotion of autonomy should be regarded as a goal to be promoted as well as possible.

Neutrality and the goal of autonomy

This immediately raises the question of how the goal of autonomy is to be optimally pursued. One natural, though not obviously correct suggestion, is that people should seek to *maximise* autonomy, rather in the way that Benthamite utilitarians seek to maximise pleasure. Some utilitarians have made the move from:

1. Pleasure is the only thing which is desirable in itself.

to

2. Actions are right in so far as they maximise pleasure.

This move may seem perfectly natural, but it is illegitimate without the inclusion of a controversial supplementary premise. Just from the fact that something is intrinsically desirable (or even the only thing which is intrinsically desirable), it doesn't follow that one should automatically seek to *maximise* it. If pleasure were the only thing which is desirable in itself, perhaps the best policy would be to try to distribute it equally. A policy of pleasure maximisation will sometimes conflict with one of pleasure equalisation, and where it does so, there is nothing in 1 which entails that it would be better to pursue the former rather than the latter, or *vice versa*.

Nevertheless, where the issue is simply one of pleasure, straightforward maximisation seems initially more appealing than where autonomy is at stake. I think this is because the value of autonomy is associated in people's minds with the view that *people* are worthy of respect, and should therefore be treated as ends in themselves. Autonomy is proposed as a value which counteracts the tendencies of some to put everything into the melting pot; people associate respect for autonomy with a rejection of Benthamite aggregations. To treat autonomy as a goal to be *maximised* is on the face of it, too close to the 'milk bottle' version of utilitarianism which regards people as of value simply in so far as they are carriers of pleasure, the invaluable elixir, which may be transferred from one container to another, to be stored in some vast bottles, and many very small ones.

Utilitarianism is a 'neutralist' philosophy in that it enjoins us to judge the rightness or wrongness of conduct from a standpoint of strict temporal and personal neutrality. Neutralism derives its strength from the following considerations: the fact that desirable state of affairs *A* occurs *at a different time* from desirable state of affairs *B* cannot directly affect their relative worth; equally, the fact that desirable experiences *C* and *D* are enjoyed by *different people* cannot directly affect *their* relative worth. According to neutralism, moral judgments should be made from a standpoint of strict impartiality – both in regard to times and to people. It is worth noting that neutralism does not have to take an 'outcome-centred' form, where conduct is judged according to its consequences. A backward-looking morality, where conduct is not judged by consequences, but rather, for example, according to whether or not rights are violated, could be equally neutralist.

Neutralist moral theory has come under attack in recent years on the grounds that it is insensitive to important facts of moral experience – notably that our characters change throughout our lives, and that a life gains its significance from the development of particular personal relations, projects and commitments.

The view that morality requires people to attempt to maximise autonomy is an example of 'neutralist consequentialism' (the view according to which the right thing to do is determined by reference to the best outcome of possible courses of action). Samuel Scheffler (1982) puts the central objection to neutralist consequentialism as follows:

'the objection arises in response to the discrepancy between the way in which concerns and commitments are *naturally* generated from a person's point of view quite independently of the weight of those concerns in an impersonal ranking of overall states of affairs, and the way in which consequentialism requires the agent to treat the concerns generated from his point of view as altogether dependent for their *moral* significance on their weight in such a ranking.' (Scheffler, 1982, p.56)

Opponents of neutralist morality are widely referred to as 'agent-relativists'. Agent-relativism is possible along either or both of two dimensions – the temporal and the personal. We have already offered some argument in favour of agent-relativism with respect to rationality – with respect to what a person has most reason to do. Sometimes it may be *rational* for an individual to act against the demands of impartial morality. Whether or not it is so depends on the person's present concerns; it may equally be rational to choose to do something which is, from a temporally neutral point of view, against one's interests. But our present concern is what *morality* requires. Here the case for neutrality is stronger. Even a fervent agent-relativist would concede that neutrality is the correct perspective for certain occasions. For example, in her capacity as a judge, nobody should allow personal bias into her rulings. Perhaps this is because one of the functions of the judiciary is to ensure that justice is done and seen to be done, in order to preserve respect for the law of the land. The present issue is over the extent of the legitimate dominion of the neutral, 'judicial' perspective.

I shall assume that there is a moral presumption in favour of neutralism, and that any exceptions to neutralist morality need to be specifically justified. My concern in the next pages is with whether or not respect for autonomy should be regarded as a neutralist value. My main strategy is to criticise what I take to be the strongest arguments against this view. After all, if autonomy is a good, then, other things equal, the more of it the better. If an equal distribution of autonomy is good, then, other things equal, the more equally autonomy is distributed the better. Any morality which enjoins people to reject neutralist principles needs a specific justification. I shall assume that autonomy should be regarded neutrally, unless there is a good reason not to.

Perhaps the most resolute contemporary agent-relativist about morality in general is Bernard Williams, who has attacked neutralism many times, for instance (1973a), (1976) and (1982). Here I shall concentrate on his argument in the (1976) paper. One of his main strategies is to argue that neutralism defeats itself in its own terms, and is therefore to be rejected.

What would, or should you do, if confronted with a fire, where it is possible to save either your spouse or two strangers, but not both? Neutralist morality would likely, in the absence of other special circumstances, declare that it would be wrong in this case, to save one's spouse. This goes against common moral feelings, although that alone does not show it to be mistaken. Williams describes, in the following words, what he takes the truth of the matter to be:

'the point is that somewhere . . . one reaches the necessity that such things as deep attachments to other persons will express themselves in the world in ways which cannot at the same time embody the impartial view, and that they also run the risk of offending against it.

They run the risk if they exist at all; yet unless such things exist, there will not be enough substance or conviction in a man's life to compel his allegiance to life itself. Life has to have substance if anything is to have sense, including adherence to the impartial system; but if it has substance, then it cannot grant supreme importance to the impartial system, and that system's hold on it will be, at the limit, insecure.' (Williams, 1976, p.215)

Insomniacs are well-advised to embark on strategies which can remove their goal of going to sleep from their consciousness. Therapists advise sexually impotent men to try to resist getting an erection, whilst being stimulated by their partners, and insomniacs to try to stay awake all night by performing boring tasks. The attempts often fail, and the therapy is successful (see Cade, 1979, p.96). Going to sleep and regaining sexual potency are not undesirable goals; it is just that their direct pursuit may be self-defeating. Williams is here claiming that the direct pursuit of the goals of impartial morality would certainly be self-defeating. For to regard all aspects of one's life as subject to justification by neutrally defensible standards would take all the spice out of life, and would give people no reason to want to go on living at all, let alone to live morally. So, whether or not one accepts neutralism at the theoretical level, as for example, characterising an ideal, one should (morally) in one's practice give weight to agent-relative concerns.

In his book *Sour Grapes: Studies in the Subversion of Rationality* (1983), Jon Elster identifies what he calls 'states that are essentially by-products'. They are those mental and social states which:

'appear to have the property that they can only come about as the by-product of actions undertaken for other ends. They can never, that is, be brought about intelligently or intentionally, because the very attempt to do so precludes the state one is trying to bring about.' (Elster, 1983, p.43)

They include, perhaps, going to sleep, impressing someone, and regaining sexual potency. Arising from the phenomenon of essentially-by-product states, there are two common 'fallacies', which Elster characterises in the following way:

'Since some of these states are useful or desirable, it is often tempting to try to bring them about – even though the attempt is certain to fall. This is the *moral fallacy of by-products*. Moreover, whenever we observe that some such state is in fact present, it is tempting to explain it as the result of action designed to bring it about – even though it is rather a sign that no such action was undertaken. This is the *intellectual fallacy of by-products*.' (Ibid., p.43)

In Elster's language Williams's position amounts to the claim that because the goals of any plausible neutralist consequentialist morality are essentially by-product states, to seek to promote them directly is to commit the moral fallacy of by-products. Williams's claim is plausible to the extent that morality develops and is sustained through the generalisation of specific concerns – notably for oneself, and family and friends. Unless these concerns develop and are sustained, human nature being what it is, it is unlikely that the more general concerns embodied within morality will have the opportunity to flourish.

However, these truths, if truths they be, do not undermine neutralist theories, including those which judge outcomes by whether or not they maximise the good (however defined). Parfit (1984) distinguishes views which are directly self-defeating from those which are merely indirectly so. Williams's argument, if successful, shows in this case, merely that neutralism may be *indirectly* self-defeating. In other words, neutral ethical goals (such as utility-maximisation), may be better realised by people being moved by non-utilitarian motives than by a more direct approach. A utilitarian may accept this without abandoning belief in utilitarian ultimate objectives. It could, with considerable plausibility, be argued that autonomy is a state which is essentially a by-product, since, for example, it is impossible to make someone act autonomously, and autonomy probably best develops in someone as a by-product of cultivating projects other than the project of becoming autonomous. However, this does not show that the neutralist goal of autonomy-promotion is misguided.

To revert to the case of the rescue: these arguments do not show that it would be *wrong* to save the two strangers rather than one's spouse. At most one can conclude that someone who chose to save her husband rather than the strangers would not incur moral blame simply because she had deliberately failed to do what was, from the perspective of neutrality, for the best. Scheffler (1982) argues for a hybrid theory, which includes agent-relative *prerogatives* (it may be morally *all right* to introduce agent-relative considerations into one's conduct), whilst rejecting *requirements* (according to which it would sometimes be *wrong* successfully to do what neutralist morality enjoined). Seriously to undermine the claim that it is right to strive to promote *autonomy* neutrally, one would need to make out a special case for agent-relative bias, which rested on the peculiarities of the value of autonomy itself.

In the paper from which I have quoted Williams writes in favour of agent-relativity in both dimensions – in the interpersonal, and in the intertemporal. His discussion of bias in the latter is particularly pertinent to autonomy and ways of recognising its importance.

To respect a person's autonomy may take the form either of promoting the development of her *capacity* for autonomy, or of promoting its *exercise* (or both). People have interests both in autonomy and in pleasant mental states, and because people may autonomously want things other than pleasant mental states, these interests may conflict. But in addition there may be an intertemporal clash of autonomy interests within a person. Throughout our lives our characters change, particularly in the sense that our values, personal commitments, overall view of the world, and basic projects, change. This means that if I give full reign to my current autonomy – exercise my autonomy to the full now, this could restrict my future autonomy, either by bringing it about that my autonomy capacity is diminished, or that opportunities for its exercise are foreclosed by present conduct. It might also lead to a very unequal distribution of autonomy through my life (which would be relevant if I thought that I should be egalitarian in regard to different phases of my life).

Suppose I take my own autonomy seriously should I try to promote it impartially throughout my whole life? Williams would answer emphatically 'No'.

He claims that a common, though damaging mistake, of much moral theory, is to exaggerate the degree to which a person's relations to his own future concerns resemble his relations to those of other people.

'The Kantian emphasis on impartiality exaggerates [the resemblance of the above relations] . . . by providing ultimately too slim a sense in which any projects are mine at all. This point . . . involves the idea that my present projects are the condition of my existence, in the sense that unless I am propelled forward by the conatus of desire, project and interest, it is unclear why I should go on at all: the world, certainly as a kingdom of moral agents, has no particular claim on my presence or, indeed, interest in it. (That kingdom, like others, has to respect the natural right to emigration).' (Williams, 1976, p.208)

And then he claims that the neutralist, neo-Kantian perspective of Rawls (1971) and Nagel (1970):

'seems . . . to imply an external view of one's own life, as something like a given rectangle that has to be optimally filled in. This perspective omits the vital consideration . . . that the continuation and size of the rectangle is up to me; so, slightly less drastically, is the question of how much of it I care to cultivate. The correct perspective on one's life is *from now*.' (Ibid., p.209)

Neutralism is supported by the principle of non-arbitrary distinctions: do not treat two cases differently unless there is a relevant difference between them. Added to this is the plausible claim that in themselves location in time and personal identity, are irrelevant to the rightness or wrongness of actions. Williams is claiming that there is a relevant difference in the life of an individual, between 'now' and the future, which apparently justifies one in not treating autonomy neutrally with respect to time.

The present is special, since, whether or not a person has a future at all depends on decisions he makes now. If a person, at any particular time, loses a sense that life is worth living, he may be tempted to end his life. It is as if myself-in-the-future has no legitimate demands on me-now, since it is entirely up to me-now, whether I-in-the-future exist at all.

This argument suggests that where there is a conflict between my present autonomy and my anticipated future autonomy interests, I should give special preference to my *present* concerns. It is therefore wrong to treat autonomy as something to be promoted neutrally throughout one's life.

The attack on neutralism with respect to other people, which claimed merely that neutralism is *indirectly* self-defeating, does not undermine the basic neutralist values. In the present case, to do serious damage to the view that autonomy should be regarded as a neutralist goal, Williams's argument needs to make a stronger claim. If it were simply an argument of the form: 'Give special weight to the present, because otherwise, any temporally neutral goals you have may be thwarted by suicide', it would be too weak for Williams's purposes. For this would make it rational for me to adopt the principle:

> Promote my autonomy through time impartially, subject to the constraint that I don't, at any time, make myself so despondent as to lose the will to live.

And this is quite different from giving special weight to the present in the way Williams advocates.

Alternatively, it could be argued that if I were to seek directly to promote my autonomy neutrally over a lifetime, I would be less autonomous than I would have been had I given, throughout my life, more weight to present concerns. This may well be true, but once again, leads only to the weaker conclusion, that the (perhaps morally best) outcome of neutral autonomy promotion within a lifetime has to be achieved by stealth. To reach Williams's conclusion, requires a much stronger claim, which gives a far more privileged position to the present perspective of the agent. One needs something like:

> Because the fate of myself-in-the-future is entirely in the hands of myself-in-the-present, the former has no legitimate claims on the latter.

And this claim seems to rest on the assumption that it is legitimate to do anything to a person over whom one has the power of life or death. This version of 'might is right' is hard to believe.

Now, rationality and morality

I argued in Chapter 3 that it is not irrational to have, and act on (at least some) temporal biases. Suppose I value my autonomy, it is not necessarily *irrational* for me to act (in pursuit of present goals) in a way which may be expected to reduce my autonomy in my life as a whole. To give an unfashionable example: It may not be irrational to enter into a binding marriage contract, although you realise at the time that this might restrict your subsequent autonomy. There are two reasons for this. First, you may value things other than autonomy. This is usually true, and interesting; but irrelevant to the present discussion. Second, and of more relevance, you might want now to give expression to the strength of your present feelings. You might have the thought 'I know it's crazy to tie myself down in this way, but that's what I really want to do, because I'm so much in love, and it would be a betrayal of my love to be moved by calculations about the future'. Here, it is plausible to say that it is a strong belief in *autonomy* which motivates the autonomy-restricting behaviour.

Someone who believes in the value of autonomy may have an agent-relative prerogative to give special weight to present autonomy. But, although this would be rational, it would equally not be obviously *irrational* for someone to refuse marriage because they cared about their autonomy (regarded neutrally across time).

The strongest case for an agent-relative restriction on the pursuit of one's own overall personal autonomy is in the field of values. People's values change, as their characters and experiences change. Some of these changes are predictable. Suppose (though this may well, as it happens, be false) that most people who are socialists at 21 become conservatives by the time they are 45. Suppose a socialist party has a long-term endowment policy, whereby I can commit myself now to paying a certain proportion of my income per year to the party, throughout my working life. This agreement could be revoked only if my financial circumstances changed dramatically for the worse. Should I sign the agreement? There is a case for saying that if I really do believe in socialism, believe that the party I am considering is the best vehicle for promoting socialism, and believe that giving financial support to the party is my best (of feasible options) way of helping the cause, then I *should* act on my *present* values, despite realising they will change. To fail to give special weight to my present values is not really to hold the values at all. Compare the above with someone who anticipates not that his *values* will change over time, but that his *beliefs* about the efficacy of giving financial aid to the party will change. If, as a result of this recognition, he decides not to enter the agreement, this is indicative of *present* doubts about the efficacy. In a sense, he doesn't really believe, even now, that giving money to the party is going to remain efficacious. Similarly, the person who fails to act on present values, because of anticipated changes in values in the distant future, doesn't really hold the values now. Of course it might be rational to have reservations about present enthusiasms, because one realises they will fade. Perhaps one believes now that there will be good reason for them to fade.

It is necessary for an agent to give special weight to his own present values and beliefs, since such a 'bias' is a precondition of having the values or beliefs at all. In this respect, from the point of view of a deliberative agent, there is a big difference between reasons coming from anticipated pleasures due, say to changes of taste, and reasons coming from anticipated changes of value. For interesting discussions of the vexed question of value-changes see Williams (1976), Parfit (1973; 1984, p.154) and Nagel (1970, p.74).

There is, then, a strong case for a 'now-agent-relative' restriction on the pursuit of one's own personal autonomy. In this respect autonomy is different from, for example, pleasure. There is no corresponding reason to give special weight to the pursuit of one's present pleasure. However, the perspective of someone thinking about another person's life is different. 'I believe that X is true, but X is false' is paradoxical, because it is not clear how I could simultaneously believe both clauses. There is no paradox, however, in sentences of the form 'He believes X, but X is false'. Similarly, in the case of evaluative beliefs, whereas 'I believe in socialism, but socialism is the worst form of social organisation' is paradoxical, the appropriate third-person formulation is not. An autonomous agent has to act, as best she can, on her present beliefs (whether moral or straightforwardly factual). However, in her benevolent dealings with others, it is not necessary that a person adopt the other's beliefs. Indeed this may be impossible.

What attitude should you, as someone concerned about the other's autonomy, take towards his present? Should you regard his autonomy through time neutrally?

Let us reconsider the socialist. Suppose the agreement needs your signature. Should you, in so far as you are concerned for my autonomy sign? There are two issues here, which need to be separated. First there is the question of whether you are a socialist. You might be motivated by your own political values. So suppose that you have no strong political views. You are indifferent between the rival political organisations. Should you, out of respect for my autonomy, help me to do what I now (autonomously) want to do, which would restrict my autonomy in my life as a whole, or should you treat my life autonomy neutrally across time?

The above arguments for 'now-agent-relativity' in the first-person case do not lead to the conclusion that it would be wrong for *you*, from the point of view of respect for *my* autonomy, to refuse to sign. Nevertheless, it may be true that refusing to sign would have the (foreseen though unintended) effect of reducing my autonomy overall, in which case a temporally neutral concern for my autonomy may rationally persuade you to sign. (Trying to maximise autonomy may, as we have seen be *indirectly* self-defeating). Moreover, refusing to sign might destroy our friendship, and you may regard our friendship as more important than my autonomy. But none of these considerations shows that in interpersonal dealings there is anything intrinsically misguided about treating the autonomy of others as a goal to be promoted neutrally across time.

Conclusion

If there were just one source of all value, then disputes which arise from conflicts between moral principles could all be settled by appeal to the grand principle. Although many philosophers, particularly utilitarians, have held that there is one such source, this view is widely contested, particularly amongst liberal thinkers. Mill's version of utilitarianism crucially differs from its original Benthamite version, in that the former recognises that the ultimate good is complex in structure. Although Mill thought that happiness is the only intrinsically valuable end, he believed it consisted not just in pleasant sensations and the absence of pain, but also in living an autonomous life.

The way in which I think the value of autonomy should be regarded is as a goal to be promoted neutrally across time and among people. I have defended this view against attacks from various quarters.

I argued first against the Kantian 'moral constraint' interpretation of the principle of respect for autonomy, which comes to grief on the rocks of moral tragedy. Where there are genuine intertemporal or interpersonal dilemmas, it is impossible not to violate someone's autonomy. As a guide to decision making in such circumstances, another principle is needed.

I then discussed whether or not the goal of autonomy promotion should be treated as an agent-relative principle. A general agent-relativist argument against ethical neutralism was shown to be uncompelling. I then argued that although there is a plausible case for saying that the attainment of autonomy is essentially a by-product, this can be accommodated by a neutralist, and it does not defeat the rationale for treating the desirability of autonomy as independent of where and to whom it occurs. Autonomy *is*, however, peculiar in that there is a sense in which people have to give special weight to their present beliefs and values; but this does not support the conclusion that such agent-relativism should be extended to interpersonal, let alone political relations.

To the extent that autonomy is desirable, it should be regarded as a neutralist goal. Whilst this does not imply that, in respect of autonomy promotion, there should be no non-neutral principles of political practice, it entails that no person's autonomy should in itself count for more than anyone else's, and that in itself, autonomy at one time is no more nor less important than autonomy at any other time. The rightness of an act of autonomy promotion, and the wrongness of one of autonomy violation are independent of to whom or when they occur.

Having just looked at how, in the most general terms, the principle of respect for autonomy should be interpreted, in the next chapter we shall address the more specific problem of how society should and should not act in regard to autonomy. This will, amongst other things, require us to take account of the fact that the attainment of autonomy amongst a population may be a state which is essentially a by-product.

7　The Liberty Principle

The story of Theseus's killing of the Minotaur ends in tragedy – the death of the hero's father, Aegeus. Theseus had agreed at the start of his voyage that, were he successful, he would hoist a white sail on his homecoming ship. If, on the other hand, he were slain, his crew would return home under the power of the original black sail. Theseus slew the Minotaur, and after various distractions and adventures, finally set sail for home. But he omitted to swap the sails. His father espied the ship in the distance, and quite rationally assumed Theseus had been killed in a failed mission; for the Minotaur was a fearsome beast, and Theseus generally kept his word. According to one version of the story, despondent, he took his own life by leaping from the Acropolis. Let us suppose you knew, it does not matter how, that Theseus was alive and successful. Benevolent concern for Aegeus would at least give you a good reason to attempt to tell him the truth about his son's mission before it was too late. But suppose you are unable to persuade him in time; for he rationally has great confidence in his son's reliability, you are a complete stranger, and in any case you do not speak the same language as the King. Under the circumstances, to delay would signify unacceptable irresolution on Aegeus's part, so there is no time to lose. What should you do?

An absolute libertarian would argue that if persuasion failed, you ought to let Aegeus plunge to his death, rather than restrict his liberty. Forcibly to stop him would be inconsistent with respect for him as an autonomous agent. This extreme position has few supporters, and most people believe that intervention, if necessary forcible intervention, would be warranted. There are at least three reasons for intervening, consistent with taking seriously a principle of respect for autonomy.

Aegeus is about to do himself great harm on the strength of a belief which you know is false. Were his son killed, suicide *would* perhaps be rational for Aegeus, and could have been an autonomous choice. However, according to the account of autonomy offered here, the choice he made was not autonomous. To prevent a person from enacting a heteronomous choice does not necessarily restrict his autonomy.

Second, we may assume that Aegeus would soon be grateful to you for your intervention because he would see the error of his belief, and would consent retrospectively to your intervention. He would come to realise that he would have asked you to intervene in this way had he known that he was going to be deceived by the black sail.

Finally, we may assume that the success of Theseus's mission would have meant that Aegeus had no reason for committing suicide, since his life would have been, even by his own standards, decidedly worth living. Indeed this is why Aegeus's death was tragic.

At the level of individual conduct, a plausible principle giving due weight to autonomy, would *have* to include a presumption in favour of allowing people to do what they want to do, except where by so doing they harm others. One part of moral theory would be to try to produce principles for determining the legitimate exceptions to this anti-paternalist presumption. I shall not offer such an account here, as our subject is *political* theory; and acceptable principles for personal life may be unacceptable in the realm of politics. But before proceeding it may be worth saying a little about the relation between moral theory, political theory and political science.

Moral theory, political theory and political science

In the last chapter I suggested that strict neutralism is indirectly self-defeating in the sense that the best way to achieve neutralist goals is to live one's life, at least in part, according to non-neutralist principles. In many circumstances these agent-relative principles will deliver the same injunctions as a neutralist counterpart. If I am out boating with just my son and he falls overboard, my weighted moral principle which allows me to give special concern to my own family's welfare enjoins me to save my son, as does a neutralist principle which gives equal weight to the welfare of all. However, there are occasions when the two conflict seriously. On these occasions it may be psychologically impossible for the person with the generally desirable (from a neutralist perspective) agent-relative concerns, to do what is required by neutralist morality, in which case, it would be inappropriate to blame the person for failing to do what is required, since 'ought' implies 'can'.

Moral theory is complex, and does not simply address itself to the question 'What ought we ideally to do?'. Parfit (1984) identifies four important facts which complicate moral theory, and to cater for these facts, five parts of moral theory. He writes:

'We must take into account these four facts:

(a) We are often uncertain what the effects of our acts will be;
(b) some of us will act wrongly;
(c) our acts are not the only effects of our motives;
(d) when we feel remorse, or blame each other, this may affect what we later do, and have other effects.' (Parfit, 1984 p.99)

The five parts of moral theory are these:

1. *Ideal Act Theory*: This states what we (the members of some group) should all ideally do, when we know that we shall all succeed.

2. *Ideal Motive Theory*: This states what motives we should all ideally have, given (a) and (c).

3. *Practical Act Theory*: This states what each of us ought to do, given (a) and (b).

4. *Practical Motive Theory*: This states what motives each of us should have, given (a), (b), and (c).

5. *Reaction Theory*: This states which are the acts for which we ought to be blamed, and should feel remorse, given (d).

Consider absolute pacifism. Is it always wrong to inflict violence on another human being? I argued in Chapter 6 that it was not.

For if some people do resort to violence, it may well be the case that the substantive aim of pacifism – the promotion of peace – is best served by committing an act of violence, as in the Huberty case. However, as part of an ideal act theory, one could still include the principle: 'Never commit an act of violence against another human being'. It is plausible to claim that if all members of a group actually managed to govern their relations with each other by this principle, the aims of pacifism would be optimally served. So it is clear how there is a need for a practical as well as an ideal act theory. It is also easy to make out a case for the other parts of moral theory distinguished by Parfit. Confusion over which part of moral theory one is discussing has led to unnecessary disagreements, particularly between utilitarian neutralists, and those who recognise the appeal of agent-relative moral principles. Parfit (1984, sections 37–40) presents a strong argument against 'ideal' agent-relative moral principles. Even if all of a group successfully act on such principles, or successfully cultivate such motives amongst its members, the result will worse achieve the moral aims of the principles themselves than would the successful following of neutralist 'ideal' principles. Such principles are 'directly self-defeating', and this is a fatal flaw.

The complexities of moral theory arise because the goals of 1 and 2 are best pursued by individuals indirectly. With political theory comes an added complication. Principles which provide the best practical guidance for individuals in their personal lives may be unacceptable as guides for conduct in the political domain. Let me try to explain why.

First consider relations between people. According to a plausible ideal act theory, actions are right if and only if they best promote the good of everyone, where each person counts equally. However, given facts (a)–(c) above, someone who accepts such an ideal act theory may subscribe to practical act and motive theories successful adherence to which leads to conduct which conflicts with that prescribed by the ideal act theory. Political theory differs here from moral theory because some facts which are especially relevant to personal conduct may be irrelevant, or less important, in the public domain, and vice versa.

Suppose it is true that ideally, everyone should, if they knew they would succeed, promote human happiness impartially. This is because, let us say, happiness is intrinsically desirable. In our imperfect world, however, it is better that individuals have agent-relative motives which are reflected in their actions than that they try to live strictly in accordance with impartial principles. One reason for this is that most people need strong personal relationships in order to retain any zest for life. Without a zest for life, it is likely that they would withdraw into a depression, and become ineffective in promoting the neutralist goal. Moreover, it may be a psychological truth about human beings that they are capable of concern for strangers only by extension of strong concerns for particular individuals. Without the latter no moral attitudes could develop, and unless specific concerns, not justified by direct appeal to neutralist principles, are maintained, there is a danger that all concern for everyone will evaporate.

Politicians and public servants are individuals. Should they, therefore, follow the principles which are laid down in our (personal) practical act and motive theories? No, because of the special responsibilities inherent in their work. These mean that they should (morally), in their professional capacity, free themselves of personal biases. Let me be more specific.

Let us assume it is acceptable for people as private individuals to have a special concern for people from their own community. Given the assortment of human fallibilities, such a pattern of biased concern may be a justifiable practical motive principle, provided the biases are not too strong.

Suppose that you care more for the citizens of your community, Alpha, than you do for citizens of another community in your country, Beta. You are a judge, and a crime has been jointly committed by a citizen of each community. You hear the case. The thought of an Alpharian spending a long time in jail distresses you more than the thought of a Betarian spending a similar time behind bars, and this is quite acceptable, morally. However, it would be wrong for you to allow this emotion to intrude into your judgment. A judge should be impartial in her public life, even though it may be right for her not to be so in her private life. This is because of the role of a judicial system, in particular, and a political system in general. One must exercise caution here, however, as there may be a big difference between the *actual* role of such a system, and that which it is *officially* supposed to fill.

On the official view, the chief role of a liberal democratic state is to promote peaceful co-operation between people, prevent violent conflict, and best to promote the interests of all its citizens. The state is necessary because people's interests conflict, and at worst, without a state apparatus there is the risk of what Hobbes called 'The war of all against all, and the life of man, solitary, poor, nasty, brutish and short'. The state mediates between different interest groups in a fair and impartial way. This is a laudable aim, consistent with, say, the goals of impartial benevolence. In order to achieve this particular aim, it is necessary for people who work for the state to free themselves of personal and sectional bias. Peaceful resolution of conflict is made easier if people believe that the decision-making procedures represent a fair compromise between conflicting interests.

According to a less rosy view, the state really represents the interests of a dominant class, and its function is always to preserve the domination of that class. In order to succeed in maintaining this 'hegemony' the ruling class seeks, either consciously or unconsciously, to convince the population at large that the political system is fair, and works, as far as possible, to the benefit of all, impartially considered. Even on this view there remain strong moral, as well as pragmatic reasons for judges to act impartially in their administration of the law.

So, on both accounts of the role of the state there are good reasons for dividing practical act and motive theories into a private and a public section. Agent-relative principles which are acceptable for individuals in the private domain may well be unacceptable in the public. This is mirrored in the field of international relations, where it may be acceptable for government ministers to act on agent-relative patriotic principles when representing their own country in negotiations, whilst it is unacceptable for them to show national bias when chairing a meeting of allies, such as the European Economic Community's Council of Ministers, or a Committee of the United Nations. One task of political theory is to establish acceptable public practical act and motive theories.

People who take on public office acquire special responsibilities which affect the principles by which they should live. The responsibilities derive in large part from the role of the political institutions within which they are working. As well as asking questions about the individual conduct of citizens in their public life, much political theory is concerned with questions about the institutional frameworks within which public figures operate, and which constrain their conduct. An extension of public practical motive theory is practical legal theory. Such a theory has to avoid the problems of, on the one hand being too abstract to be of any relevance to practical affairs, and on the other, of becoming too bogged down in the analysis of a particular complex concrete situation.

One telling criticism (due in the first instance to Karl Marx) of much political theory of the seventeenth, eighteenth and nineteenth centuries is that it has made the error of mistaking local conditions of humanity for universal truths. The result of this mistake is to make the theories excessively conservative. A prime example is Thomas Hobbes (1588–1679).

In his major work *Leviathan* Hobbes put forward the thesis that because of the fundamental selfishness of human beings it is essential that there be a strong government with a monopoly of force in any society. The reason for this is that without such a power, individuals will always be subject to threat from other individuals. It is necessary to have a strong government in order to provide people with incentives to refrain from stealing, physical violence and murder. He argued that in a 'state of nature', a form of existence without civil society and government, there would be a continuous war of all against all, with a complete breakdown of security for those unfortunate enough to live at all.

Hobbes's mistake was to claim, with quite inadequate evidence, that what was plausibly true of people in a specific historical context, seventeenth-century England, was universally true – of all people at all times. Perhaps people in the England of the Civil War period needed a strong central government in order to prevent a state of perpetual war of all against all. It does not follow that all people, at all times, must have such a need (see Macpherson, 1962). Indeed, it is the contention of socialist thinkers, that people are not innately selfish in Hobbes's sense, but have the capacity for genuinely uncoerced co-operation, if only the social conditions are right. In such a community of suitably transformed human beings, the welfare of all would be a precondition of the welfare of each. This transformation of human nature may be possible, but only through the transformation of class-divided society (where the means of creating wealth are owned by one group, from which outsiders are by and large excluded).

The lesson to be drawn from these considerations is that political theorists should be prepared to relativise many of their proposals to particular historical situations. Hobbes could be construed as offering practical principles which are apposite for seventeenth-century England. Given that there are many huge differences between England then and modern Britain or North America, one would expect that some different principles would apply to each. This is not, of course, to rule out in principle the possibility of any universal principles, but merely to state that it is dangerous, as well as tempting, to propose them by generalising from one's own local conditions.

If there are any universal principles of this type, their discovery is one task for political science. So, political theory is bounded on one side by personal moral theory, and on the other by political science. A distinctive role of a political theorist is to link the two, in producing practical public act and motive theories, and a practical legal theory.

The state and individual liberty

I have argued that there are occasions when it is impossible to avoid violating somebody's autonomy. This is true for both private individuals and public agents. The example of Aegeus will convince most readers that there are occasions when it may be justifiable for an individual private citizen to restrain the actions of another in order to protect the other from harm. The fact that many people have strong desires not to be restricted, combined with uncertainties, and the fact that we may have dubious motives for controlling the lives of our fellows, are sufficient to justify a strong presumption, in our practical principles, in favour of not interfering with people's liberty to live their own lives and make their own mistakes. However, it is justifiable to adopt principles which enable us to intervene on some occasions – either to protect other parties, or to protect the agent in question. Should similar ground rules apply to the conduct of public as well as private citizens? Mill, one of the staunchest defenders of the liberty of the individual, thought not. He proposed a far stronger restriction on the powers of the state to interfere in the private lives of its citizens.

At the heart of Mill's political theory is the following practical act principle for public agents:

'the sole end for which mankind are warranted, individually or collectively, in interfering with the liberty of action of any of their number, is self-protection . . . the sole purpose for which power can be rightfully exercised over any member of a civilised community, against his will, is to prevent harm to others. His own good, either physical or moral, is not a sufficient warrant. He cannot rightfully be compelled to do or forbear because it will be better for him to do so, because it will make him happier, because, in the opinion of others, to do so would be wise, or even right. These are good reasons for remonstrating with him, or reasoning with him, or persuading him, or entreating him, but not for compelling him, or visiting him with any evil in case he do otherwise . . . The only part of the conduct of any one which is amenable to society, is that which concerns others. In the part which merely concerns himself, his independence is, of right, absolute. Over himself, over his own body and mind, the individual is sovereign.' (Mill, 1859, pp.72–3)

Although this famous statement refers to individual as well as collective conduct, I do not think it is proposed as a part of private practical act theory. Mill is not saying that it is legitimate for a person *to stop a friend* from harming herself *only* in order to prevent attendant harm to other people. The subject-matter of the essay *On Liberty* is 'the dealings of society with the individual', and the above quotation is making a statement about the conduct of people in their capacity as citizens.

Mill believed that in their public capacity people should exercise such a strong restraint on their own benevolent interference with the conduct of fellow citizens, because he thought that the fundamental goal of 'the general happiness' would be best served by a complete institutional ban on purportedly benevolent interference with the private life of individuals, together with an accompanying self-denying ordinance among public servants.

On a traditional interpretation of Mill, his adherence to the neo-absolutist Liberty Principle, quoted above, has always been something of a mystery. It is well known that Mill was a utilitarian, which is a neutralist, consequentialist morality. How could he reconcile his utilitarianism with a belief in the Liberty Principle? The traditional view is that Mill was torn between the utilitarianism he had been brought up to accept, and a passionate belief in liberty – the two ultimately being in conflict. In his important account of Mill's views on liberty, Gray (1983) has offered an interpretation of Mill which shows that the writings on liberty are after all consistent with Mill's utilitarianism. The version of utilitarianism which emerges from this interpretation is attractive, especially to those who recognise the importance of autonomy. Gray offers a detailed account in defence of his interpretation of Mill, and I refer the reader to Gray's book for a full exposition of Mill's views on liberty. I shall here offer my own sketch of a view, which though possibly not exactly Mill's own, is certainly Millian.

First we have what Gray calls 'the axiological principle of utility':

1. Happiness is desirable, and the only thing which is desirable as an end in itself.

The concept 'happiness' has, certainly since the ancient Greeks, been a source of controversy. I think that Mill's conception of happiness differed from that of his mentor, Bentham, and in fact has much in common with Aristotle's. The Aristotelian conception of *eudaimonia*, which means something like 'flourishing' or 'well-being', is perhaps closest to the Millian conception to which I am attracted. Some of Mill's writings clearly suggest that this was his view, whereas others suggest he was actually wedded to something more like the Benthamite conception. In so far as Mill had two views of happiness, I am focusing on his more Aristotelian conception – as more pertinent to our discussion of autonomy.

Mill disagreed with crude hedonists who identified happiness with an exceedingly pleasant mental feeling. He did not believe that happiness is a life of permanent exalted pleasure. On the contrary, he describes happiness as:

'not a life of rapture; but moments of such, in an existence made up of few and transitory pains, many and various pleasures, with a decided predominance of the active over the passive, and having as the foundation of the whole, not to expect more from life than it is capable of bestowing. A life thus composed, to those who have been fortunate enough to obtain it, has always appeared worthy of the name of happiness. And such an existence is even now the lot of many, during some considerable portion of their lives. The present wretched education, and wretched social arrangements, are the only real hindrance to its being attainable by almost all.' (Mill, 1861, p.12)

Happiness, then, is a state which it is possible for (almost all) people to attain, given the right social conditions (about which there is great controversy).

Next there is a principle stating what the ultimate aim of a civil society should be:

2. The ultimate aim of a civil society should be to promote the general happiness.

That is to say, the ultimate aim of a society should be to bring it about that happiness is as 'general' as possible. In other words, the aim should be to make as many people as possible 'happy', or bring them to a state where they are flourishing as people. Happiness is a satisfiable goal, in that it is possible for a person simply to become happy, or at least sufficiently happy that any further improvement in her happiness is of little or no moral value compared to her reaching that level of happiness (we might compare happiness, so conceived, with health). So the aim of the general happiness has built into it an egalitarian principle according to which the top priority is to enable as many people as possible to attain happiness. This is, of course, on Mill's assumption that happiness is attainable by most, if not all people. If one believed that happiness was attainable by only a few people, then one might argue that the top priority was to ensure that at least *they* attained happiness, even if this meant that others, well below the level of happiness, were worse off than they could otherwise be. As I have stressed, Mill certainly thought

happiness was in principle attainable by (nearly) all, and I think
one has to assume it is, in order to make sense of liberal arguments
for broad political participation and the passionate defence of
negative liberty so close to the heart of liberalism.

Next, there is a theory of vital interests. Vital interests are
those interests which must be satisfied by anyone in order to
flourish, or attain happiness.

3. Human beings have vital interests in security and autonomy.

As we saw in Chapter 5, Mill believed that people do not share
all the same interests, because we may be constituted differently,
are shaped by different life experiences, live distinct lives, and
are fascinated by different things. Being rational creatures, we
have the capacity not only to discover and pursue, but also to
transform our own needs and interests. However, in order to
achieve happiness, it is necessary for anyone that he or she has
the security of reliable established expectations. Mill describes
security as:

> 'the most vital of all interests. All other benefits are needed by
> one person, not needed by another, and many of them can, if
> necessary, be cheerfully forgone, or replaced by something
> else, but security no human being can possibly do without; on
> it we depend for all our immunity from evil, and for the whole
> value of all and every good, beyond the passing moment; since
> nothing but the gratification of the instant could be of any
> worth to us, if we could be deprived of anything the next
> instant by whoever was momentarily stronger than ourselves.'
> (Ibid., p.50)

Autonomy is a vital interest not only because it is usually a
means to the other ingredients of happiness, but also because it is
a constituent of happiness itself. In order for anything like Mill's
Liberty Principle to be plausible, this has to be recognised. For if
happiness were simply equivalent to being in a perpetually
pleasant mental state, it could be achieved in principle by plugging
people into an experience machine, or drugging them. Their
liberty would be irrelevant. Once again, just as happiness is a
satisfiable goal, so is autonomy. It is, as we saw earlier, impossible

for anyone to become completely autonomous; however, in so far as happiness is a satisfiable goal and autonomy is a precondition of happiness, there is a level of autonomy which is attainable, and is such that, beyond it, any further increases in autonomy are of little or no moral value compared with the value of attaining it. For one's life to be good enough that one flourishes or is happy, it is necessary to have reached a certain level of self-determination or autonomy. We may call this state 'being autonomous'.[1]

Mill's claim that people have a vital interest in autonomy ultimately rests on the plausible belief that (nearly all) those who are aware of what autonomy is, would not be prepared to sacrifice their autonomy for even large increases in other pleasures. We have already seen that Mill's argument for the view that everyone has a vital interest in autonomy, is inconclusive. However, if the prime purpose of society *is* to promote the general happiness, and autonomy *is* a necessary condition of happiness, then society should have as an aim the promotion of autonomy amongst its citizens. Hence the fourth part of the theory states that autonomy should be promoted by society.

4. Society should have as an aim the promotion of the general autonomy.

Just as 'the general happiness' means 'the happiness of all', so what I have called 'the general autonomy' means 'the autonomy of all'. This is an egalitarian principle which I think is the most plausible way of incorporating the Kantian principle of respect for persons within a broadly utilitarian framework. The principle of equal respect for persons is central to the moral justification of liberalism.

It should be noted that 4 does not entail that autonomy promotion should be enshrined in legislation, or even be regarded as a *direct* concern of society; merely that 'the general autonomy' should be an ultimate objective of society, and that societies can be judged by considering how widespread autonomy is amongst its population – by asking how many people in the society are autonomous.

---

[1] For the idea of treating happiness and autonomy as 'satisfiable goals' I am indebted to correspondence with John Baker, and to his unpublished paper 'Finite Utilitarianism'.

Next there is a series of factual claims about the conditions for the development and maintenance of autonomy in human beings, and about the fallibility of public opinion and governments. These include:

5a. Autonomy develops only in those who are allowed to practice making their own decisions, even when such decisions may be unwise.

5b. On the whole people know their own interests better than do other people.

5c. Unless there is a sphere of life which is protected from the force of public opinion and other social pressures, individual development will be stifled, and people will settle into a dull conformity.

5d. People have a strong preference not to have their liberty restricted by public institutions.

5e. Those in positions of power are easily led into thinking that actions which serve their own interests and work against those over whom they have power, actually do serve the latter's interests.

As a result of these factual claims, we finally arrive at a strong principle of liberty, which has, as its rationale, utilitarianism.

6. The protection of citizens from harm which they might do themselves should not be a function of a civilised society in dealings with its citizens.

Leaving aside difficulties which there undoubtedly are with adequately defining 'civilised', one can easily see a rationale for the restriction contained within the principle. People have vital interests in both security and autonomy. In one sense the former interest is more basic. If one lacked security totally, there would be no possibility of developing autonomy, whereas one could gain security without autonomy. Autonomy becomes the most pressing vital interest once basic security is established.

The plausibility of 6 is derived from acceptance of the view that autonomy is a vital interest, and a recognition that the instruments of the state are relatively blunt, unable to make distinctions even as finely-tuned as those available to individuals. It is intended to cover both coercive social pressure, and more specifically, the law. Just as our private acts are not the only effects of our motives, so too the acts of public politicians and officials are not the only effects of laws. It may sometimes be morally right to refuse to pass legislation which outlaws certain immoral behaviour, whilst it may equally be morally right to pass legislation which prevents public agents from performing actions which were they performed by individuals as private citizens would be morally acceptable. The Liberty Principle should be regarded as a public practical motive principle, and as the grounds for a practical legal principle banning, at least certain forms of, state paternalism.

The general problem

The Liberty Principle, interpreted in the above way, has more plausibility than it is sometimes credited with. The standard objection to the principle is that there are occasions where a specific violation of the principle would undoubtedly have, on balance, good consequences. These consequences could either be the prevention of pain, the promotion of pleasure, or the promotion of autonomy.

Mill attempts to deal with this sort of objection to his general principle in a famous passage concerning an imprudent bridge crosser:

> 'it is a proper office of public authority to guard against accidents. If either a public officer or anyone else saw a person attempting to cross a bridge which had been ascertained to be unsafe, and there were no time to warn him of his danger, they might seize him and turn him back without any real infringement of his liberty; for liberty consists in doing what one desires, and he does not desire to fall into the river.' (Mill, 1859, pp.151–2)

I think most would agree that under the circumstances Mill describes it would be right to prevent the person from walking onto the bridge, by force as a last resort if necessary. However, Mill's treatment of this case is unsatisfactory.

The first problem is that seizing the man and turning him back really would be an infringement of his liberty. You would be forcibly preventing him from doing something which he clearly wanted to do.

What is special about this case is that the prevented action would have had an immediate consequence which, one assumes, is unknown to the prospective agent, and is such that, were he aware of it, he would not have wanted to step onto the bridge. To the extent that his action is motivated by the false belief that the bridge is safe, his autonomy in regard to the decision about whether or not to step onto it is impaired, as was that of Aegeus when he leaped from the Acropolis. Preventing him from stepping onto the bridge does not stop him from exercising his autonomy; nor does it cast doubt on his status as an autonomous citizen (there is no presumption that he generally lacks the ability to run his own life, or that he should be prevented from exercising this capacity).

This suggests that the Liberty Principle should be interpreted so as to sanction what is called 'weak paternalism', whilst proscribing 'strong paternalism'. The former permits the restriction of liberty to prevent people from harming themselves, in cases where the harm would be the result of the person having false beliefs about the consequences of his action. After all, forcibly restraining the incautious bridge crosser does not threaten his sovereignty over his own life. Which goals he has and pursues remains up to him. One is not seeking to deny people the freedom to take decisions which appear to (and may actually) be against their interests, provided the decision is not taken in ignorance. Mill wrote:

> 'when there is not a certainty, but only a danger of mischief, no one but the person himself can judge of the sufficiency of the motive which may prompt him to incur the risk: in this case, therefore (unless he is a child, or delirious, or in some state of excitement or absorption incompatible with the full use of the reflecting faculty), he ought, I conceive, to be only warned of the danger; not forcibly prevented from exposing himself to it.'
> (Ibid., p.152)

The reason it is all right forcibly to prevent the man from stepping onto the bridge is that there is no time to warn him of the danger, and it is certain that he will be harmed if he steps on to the bridge. One may reasonably assume, in the absence of specific evidence to the contrary, that he would not step onto the bridge if he realised the danger of so doing. This is quite different from a case where someone steps onto the bridge, aware of its danger, either because he doesn't mind taking the risk, or because, for some reason, he wants to fall into the river. In this case restraint by force would be an example of impermissible strong paternalism – the imposition of goals upon the agent – a violation of his sovereignty over his own life.

Interpreting the Liberty Principle so that it sanctions weak, but not strong paternalism certainly makes it more plausible; but still further problems of interpretation remain. Mill says that 'when there is not a certainty, but only a danger of mischief' befalling an agent, it is up to the agent to choose whether she wants to take the risk. But how strictly should we interpret this? The consequences of all actions are uncertain to a degree. Is it wrong forcibly to prevent someone playing Russian roulette with a gun which (unknown to the player) really *does* contain a live bullet? It seems that certainty of mischief is hardly relevant here, where what is crucial is the agent's ignorance. It is well-known that cigarette smoking and high-fat diets carry a risk of serious health hazards. It is also known that many people, in spite of health education and warnings, really are ignorant of these risks. Should they be banned from smoking and eating high-fat foods? Such a ban would certainly go against the spirit of the Liberty Principle, as well as its letter. Again, Mill states that it may be legitimate forcibly to prevent a person from exposing himself to danger if 'he is a child, or delirious, or in some state of excitement or absorption incompatible with the full use of the reflecting faculty'. This immediately raises the question of what it might be about children that makes them a suitable target for paternalism. It also raises the problem of how to interpret 'full use of the reflecting faculty'. After all, nobody is perfectly rational, and most decisions are taken in the light of people's present interests and commitments (absorptions?).

It is clear, then, that the interpretation of the Liberty Principle, or that of a suggested alternative, is likely to be controversial and inconclusive. The motivational and legal restrictions on the extent of legitimate state interest in the lives of individuals, implied by the Liberty Principle, are justified, if at all, by the fact, if it is a fact, that adhering to them provides an optimal route towards the goal of the general happiness (which includes the general autonomy). The fact that there are occasions when the policy of strict adherence leads to an action which would be worse (in terms of the goals which provide its rationale) than an alternative which would require the restrictions to be broken, does not undermine the reason for adopting the policy; the fact that acting on agent-relative motives sometimes is non-optimal, does not destroy the rationale for developing such motives. In the field of individual conduct total flexibility of motive is impossible, and within a system of public institutions, even less flexibility is possible. This does suggest that a neo-absolutist protection of a private sphere of liberty is likely to be justifiable, although, as the above considerations suggest, its boundaries may be hard to define.

It is very difficult to test a principle as general as the Liberty Principle, which is justified by consequentialist considerations. The principle is theoretically falsifiable, relative to a particular conception of happiness. It would be falsified if it could be shown that the goal of the general happiness could be better served by the acceptance of a rival principle. However, this would be very hard to show, since the principle's acceptability is consistent with the existence of individual cases where it leads to the performance of actions which do not optimally promote the substantive goals which give it its rationale. For the only conditions under which it may be empircially possible to perform the preferred act would presuppose laws or motives which, on balance, produce worse consequences than a strict adherence to the Principle.

Conclusion

In this chapter I have identified the attempt to produce public practical act and motive theories, and a practical legal theory as key tasks of political theory. I have given some attention to Mill's famous Liberty Principle, as it gives a clear expression of a liberal attitude towards taking autonomy seriously in the political realm. The main rationale for the principle derives from the two claims – that autonomy is a vital constituent of happiness, and that autonomy is best promoted by adherence to the restrictions of the Principle in the formation of legislation, in the conduct of public officers in their official capacities, and in those who shape the boundaries of the acceptable area for the influence of public opinion. Both claims are controversial, since the former is contingent on interpretations of two highly controversial concepts, whereas the latter is perhaps *practically* untestable.

Rather than try further to defend the conceptions of autonomy and happiness offered here, I shall, in the third section of this book, take them for granted. For I believe they are not only plausible, but perhaps more importantly, are the conceptions which make sense of the passionate belief in individual (negative) liberty which is characteristic of liberal democratic society.

Rather than try to test the Liberty Principle, or produce and test rival theories of equal generality, I shall apply the liberal value of respect for autonomy to three specific problems where there is a *prima facie* conflict between the Liberty Principle and the value. My purpose is not so much to test the Liberty Principle, as to test liberal democratic society by the criteria of its own manifest standards.

The problems I shall discuss concern children, the mentally disordered, and false consciousness. They are all of particular interest to liberal political theory, because children and the mentally disordered are *minorities* whose autonomy is widely held to be seriously impaired, whereas radical socialists believe that the autonomy of the *majority* is impaired by false consciousness.

PART III

PRACTICES

So far we have discussed rival conceptions of autonomy, and considered in an abstract way, how autonomy could be taken seriously as a value in society. In this part of the book we shall examine more specific practical problems for liberal democratic society.

A distinguishing feature of the values of liberal democracy is that individual autonomy is regarded as of vital importance – not just as a means to further ends, but for its own sake – as a constituent of human happiness or well-being. A prime goal of liberal democracy is to produce a society composed of autonomous citizens who would work and play productively and co-operatively, motivated by their individual conceptions of a good life. However, individuals' exercise of autonomy could legitimately be restricted if this is necessary to protect the rights of others. In no society should someone be allowed to kill another just because he didn't like the look of his face. It is, in a just society, legitimate to restrict liberty only for the sake of liberty itself. (For a discussion on this principle, see Rawls, 1971, Chapter 4).

A central tenet of liberalism is that people should be allowed and indeed encouraged autonomously to discover and pursue their own individual ends, provided they do not thereby prevent others from discovering and pursuing theirs. But what about people who are demonstrably not autonomous? Should they be allowed just to live their lives as they choose, provided they do not thereby injure other people? It seems obvious that they should not. But attempts to justify such restrictions run into difficulties. It may be difficult to reconcile the liberal passion for liberty with what seems to be justifiable paternalism towards the less-than-autonomous.

Rather than discuss these dilemmas in general terms, in this part of the book we shall consider three categories of people who for one reason or another, may be thought to have seriously limited autonomy. We shall first discuss children and the mentally disordered, two groups whose autonomy is impaired. We shall then consider problems associated with the view, held notably by some radical socialists, that the majority of the population suffer from autonomy impairment in virtue of being victims of 'false consciousness'.

8   Children

'If you're bored, you learn only how to be
bored. Whether the timetable says maths,
geography, or whatever.

If you have to do as you're told all the time,
all you learn is to be obedient and not to
question things. You learn not to think.

If you're forced to learn, you learn that
learning is unpleasant. It's no help that the
teacher says it will come in useful later in
life.' (*The Little Red School Book*)

'paternalistic interference must be justified by the evident
failure or absence of reason and will; and it must be guided by
the principles of justice and what is known about the subject's
more permanent aims and preferences, or by the account of
primary goods.' (John Rawls)

In the paragraph immediately succeeding his statement of the
Liberty Principle, which speaks of the complete sovereignty of
the individual over his own life, Mill wrote the following:

'It is perhaps hardly necessary to say that this doctrine is meant
to apply only to human beings in the maturity of their faculties.
We are not speaking of children, or of young persons below the
age which the law may fix as that of manhood or womanhood.
Those who are still in a state to require being taken care of by
others must be protected against their own actions as well as
against external injury.' (Mill, 1859, p.73)

Mill's disclaimer certainly seems to have been widely accepted,
even by those who are sympathetic to the spirit of the Liberty

Principle. Paternalistic 'protection' of children is pursued by legislators, social policy makers, teachers, other public servants, and within the family.

I have spoken of the importance of autonomy within liberal democracy. How is recognition of this value to be reconciled with the special treatment given to 'minors'. The restrictions imposed on children are great, as John Harris (1982) has forcefully stated in a paper by which I have been influenced:

> 'In addition to the long list of political and legal disabilities imposed on children – inability to vote, to initiate or defend legal proceedings on their own account, consent to sexual relations and so on – they are also positively controlled and their lives almost completely regulated by adults . . . This control finds dramatic and public expression and reinforcement in the system of compulsory attendance at and obedience in schools.' (Harris, 1982, p.35)

Although this description is tendentious, and the claim that children's lives are 'almost completely regulated by adults' is probably an exaggeration, there is enough truth in Harris's statement to present a serious challenge to a defender of the liberal tradition.

In this chapter I shall examine what I call 'the received view' in the light of principles about autonomy, which I take to be crucial to the moral defence of the liberal democratic societies exemplified by North America, the United Kingdom and Australasia.

The received view

According to the received view children are a legitimate exception to anti-paternalistic principles because they lack the abilities and experience which make it wrong to impose decisions on *adults* for their own sake. Children are said to lack the ability to make rational choices, and certainly the experience to make wise ones. Because of this deficiency, taking decisions on their behalf, such as compelling them to attend school, or forbidding them to enter into contracts, does not violate their autonomy; for they clearly lack autonomy, and restricting their liberty is consistent with acceptable principles of weak paternalism. Restrictions on children are necessary for their own good in general, and specifically to enable them to develop their potential as adults. Far from being inconsistent with a respect for autonomy, paternalism towards children is required by a genuine concern for their autonomy.

In the nineteenth century far-reaching paternalistic legislation was introduced ostensibly to protect the interests of children. However, it is clear that the changes were often prompted by other needs. Consider, for example, this recent account of the 1870 Education Act which made education compulsory in Britain:

'much of the value of a national education lay outside its ability to educate. Education was important in removing from the streets and alleyways those children who had so plagued society and taxed the popular imagination . . . To have all the nation's children in the classrooms during much of the working day, throughout a substantial part of the year, fulfilled a number of important social roles. After a fashion it brought the children under control, it expanded employment opportunities, particularly for young women, and permitted parents and relatives to escape from the tedious tasks of child-minding to take up paid employment. Admittedly these consequences had little educational justification though, in time, they were to become powerful arguments in themselves. Nonetheless, they were very real consequences of the education system which had developed by 1900.' (Walvin, 1982, p.122)

If this is right it is likely that the educational needs of children did not constitute the main reason for the passing of the 1870 Act. More important was the fact that the streets were overrun with roving children, women were seeking employment, and all in all it was socially necessary for the well-being of *adults*, that children be made to attend school. Of course, to offer such a materialistic explanation for the success of attempts to introduce these educational reforms, is not to cast doubt on the sincerity of the concern for children expressed by supporters of compulsory schooling. It is, however, potentially challenging to the moral justification for the legislation, and may weaken the case for preserving compulsion today.

Respect for children

According to the Millian view, which I take to be central to the moral justification of liberal democracy, autonomy is a vital interest (essential ingredient of human happiness, flourishing or well-being). It is this supposition which makes best sense of liberal beliefs in civil liberties and anti-paternalistic restrictions on the role of the state in civilised society.

One of the conclusions of Chapter 6 was that, despite arguments to the contrary, autonomy, like pleasure and the avoidance of pain, should be regarded as a neutralist goal. In other words, the moral cost or benefit of any given loss or gain in any person's autonomy is directly independent of to whom it accrues, and when it occurs. This means that in principle anyone's autonomy is as morally significant as anyone else's, and also that autonomy in one period of a person's life is in itself no more nor less important than autonomy at any other stage.

In Chapter 7 I endorsed the view that happiness is a satisfiable goal in that it is possible for people to become happy *simpliciter* (that is, reach a state of flourishing), or at least sufficiently happy that any further improvement in their happiness is of little or no moral value compared to that of their reaching that level of happiness. If this is accepted, then a top priority of society should be to ensure that as many of its people as possible reach that desirable state. To permit some to live at a higher level than (mere) happiness at the expense of those who are thereby kept below this level, is to violate the principle of treating people as ends in themselves, which distinguishes liberalism from, amongst other things, crude versions of classical utilitarianism.

Because autonomy is a vital interest it is more important that nobody should be more than merely happy if the cost is that there are some people whose autonomy is kept at a level lower than that which is required for happiness. Again, compare with health. It is more important that everyone reaches a certain level of health, which we can call 'becoming healthy' than that some, who are already healthy, become super-healthy.

The morality which supports liberal democracy requires that equal respect be shown to all people. Before addressing the question of whether children are accorded less respect than, as people, they should be, it is necessary to answer a prior question: 'Are children people at all?' This is not as strange as it sounds.

Are children people?

As it has been used in philosophy 'person' is a term of art which designates those who have what it takes to be members of the moral community. One would therefore expect disagreement about who or what are, in the relevant sense, people.

In debates about the morality of abortion, those opposed to abortion sometimes speak of the principle of an equal right to life. They claim that all people have an equal right to life, whether they are adults, children, or embryos in the womb. Against them it may be argued that, although (human) embryos and foetuses are *human* beings, as opposed to, say, *dog* foetuses, they are not people. To be a person is to have abilities which foetuses certainly lack. Therefore important moral principles which apply to people do not apply to foetuses.

As far as *this* argument goes, the defender of a woman's right to choose is on firmer ground than her opponent. For in the context of liberal theory, going back certainly to Kant, the principle of respect for people does rest on claims that there is something special about people – namely that we are creatures with a will, not merely non-rational animals (see Chapter 2). If it is in virtue of this that humanity should be treated as an end in itself, then presumably the requirement applies to all and only rational creatures, whom we may designate 'people', whether or not they are human. Human foetuses lack these qualities and so are not people in the sense which is most natural to defenders of the principle of respect for people, although they may, given favourable circumstances, become people. In Kant's words:

'Beings whose existence depends, not on our will, but on nature, have . . . if they are non-rational beings, only a relative value as means and are consequently called *things*. Rational beings, on the other hand, are called *persons* because their nature already marks them out as ends in themselves – that is, as something which ought not to be used merely as a means – and consequently imposes to that extent a limit on all arbitrary treatment of them (and is an object of reverence).' (Kant, 1785, p.91)

If foetuses are not people, whereas normal adults are, the question arises, 'When, in its life history, does a human being become a person?' It would seem that it becomes a person when it ceases to be non-rational. Although there are degrees of irrationality, there are not degrees of non-rationality. Stones are not more non-rational than ants, even though the behaviour of ants more closely approximates that of a rational creature than does the behaviour of stones. In this sense rationality/non-rationality is an all-or-none concept. To be a person is, in this respect like being inside a circle, though admittedly the boundaries of a circle are clear, whereas it may not be clear whether or not someone is a person. What are the criteria for being a person?

Certainly consciousness is a requirement. More specifically, a person is a creature which has beliefs and desires, and acts on its desires in the light of its beliefs. However, this is insufficient for personhood. What is required in addition is the capacity to evaluate and structure one's beliefs and desires, and to act on the basis of these evaluations. A creature could be minimally rational, in the sense that it acted on its beliefs and desires, efficiently, to satisfy the desires; but it would not be a person, if it lacked the capacity to question the worthwhileness of the desires, and the soundness of the beliefs.

In Chapter 5 we considered Frankfurt's account of freedom of the will and the concept of a person. According to Frankfurt, in order to be a person, a creature must have second-order volitions – that is desires about which of her desires she wants to become her will. In order for a person to have a free will, her will must be as she wants it to be, that is, her actual motivating desires are the desires she overall wants to motivate her. People in this sense, have wills, in so far as they do not necessarily act on their strongest inclinations, but have the general ability to act on the results of their deliberation.

This account of people and free will has much to commend it. It gives a clear sense to the notion of a free will, and it draws an appropriate connection between the Kantian notion of beings with 'dignity', and freedom of the will. How do children come out on this view?

No creature, whether human or not, is a person, unless it possesses second-order volitions, and certainly it is implausible to attribute second-order volitions to foetuses or babies. So neither foetuses nor babies are people. But what is presupposed by the capacity to have second-order volitions?

I think a crucial requirement is possession of the concept of a self. In order to have second-order volitions, someone has to be able to think of himself as a being with a future and a past, a subject of experiences, a possessor of beliefs and desires. It may not be clear exactly when children acquire these abilities; perhaps they are acquired gradually, and cases may arise where it is not obvious whether a child has sufficiently acquired the requisite concepts to be a person.

We can say, I think without being too controversial, that by the age of 7 it is not uncommon for children to be people. A child goes to school, and feels shy. The shyness manifests itself as a desire not to speak to other children. And yet the shy child does want not to be shy, he wants to make his desire to speak to the other children into his will; but painfully, he is not able to do this, and his will is not free. After a while there is a breakthrough, and he is able to overcome his shyness, and put into practice his second-order volition.

It is certainly true that by 10 years of age, non-mentally-handicapped children are people, even in Frankfurt's rather restrictive sense. Moreover, in England, 10 is the age at which it is supposed children become criminally responsible for their actions. Children of this age certainly are fit subjects for the Kantian principle of respect.

The conception of a person which I have outlined above is probably more restrictive than most, in that it does exclude numbers of human beings from the category 'person'. However, even *it* would definitely include as people non-mentally-handicapped children of 10 and over. So, to simplify matters I shall restrict my comments to the treatment of non-mentally-handicapped children of 10 and over, leaving for another occasion further discussion of just when children do become people. Many restrictions are placed on the liberty of children over 10, which definitely do not apply to adults. Are these restrictions compatible with respect for them as people – in particular with respect for their autonomy?

Neutralist morality requires that there should be no arbitrary discrimination against any person or class of people. Are children discriminated against? Are the special limitations on the freedom of children unfair and arbitrary? The majority of writers follow Mill in maintaining that restrictions on the liberty of children are justifiable.

Mill, as we have seen, specifically excluded children from his Liberty Principle, on the grounds that those who still require being taken care of by others 'must be protected against their own actions as well as against external injury'. In the style of a true citizen of Victorian England, he extends this paternalistic principle to 'those backward states of society in which the race itself may be considered as in its nonage', thinking of some 'races' as in just as much need of 'protection' as children.

But what *is* the principle by which one can judge whether an individual or society is not yet ready to make its own life-affecting decisions? Mill writes:

'Liberty, as a principle, has no application to any state of things anterior to the time when mankind have become capable of being improved by free and equal discussion . . . as soon as mankind have attained the capacity of being guided to their own improvement by conviction or persuasion . . . compulsion, either in the direct form or in that of pains and penalties for non-compliance, is no longer admissible as a means to their own good, and justifiable only for the security of others.' (Mill, 1859, pp.74–5)

Many children (by this, in what follows I mean non-mentally-handicapped children of over 10 years) are apparently not capable of being improved by free and equal discussion. But on the other hand, there are many *adults* who aren't either. Moreover, there are some children who clearly *are* capable of being improved in this manner. If the Liberty Principle applies to all and only those with an ability, such as the one that Mill specifies, then it seems arbitrary to withhold its application in a blanket way to all people under a certain age, whilst extending it to others, who differ not in respect of the ability, but simply through being older.

An interesting comparison could be drawn here with racist restrictions. Suppose it were true that on average the members of one racial group were less well-qualified in medicine than those of another group. This gives no justification for barring members of the former group from practising medicine. At the very least, competition for places in medical school should be open to those from the disadvantaged group who were no less able than those of the other group, who were accepted at medical school. To deny individuals places on the grounds that they come from a group which is, on average, less able than another, is to discriminate unfairly against those individuals.

As I have already said, children's liberty is severely curtailed, when compared with that of adults. To examine the charge that these restrictions amount to discrimination against children, I shall consider two areas where children's liberty is restricted – the vote, and education; although I could have equally chosen sexual behaviour, contract law, choice of abode, employment, or any of a number of others. However, each case would require some detailed argument, as each generates its own special problems.

Before embarking on a discussion of the vote and education, it is worth mentioning that the mere fact that children are treated differently from adults does not mean that there is unfair or arbitrary discrimination. It does not, for example, violate the principle to offer special mobility allowances to the physically handicapped, who are unable to walk. The fact that some people (including children) may have special needs really can legitimise differential treatment – in the name of equal respect for all. However, the onus is always on those who favour differential treatment in a particular case, to prove their point.

The vote

Certainly since the English Civil War there have been moves to extend the franchise; first from just the male aristocracy to male property owners; then eventually to all males over 21; to all men over 21 and to rather older women; to all men and women over 21, and most recently, to everyone over 18 (with a few notable exceptions, including, among others, the mentally disordered). In a liberal democracy governments are elected with the support of a wide range of interest groups – namely those amongst the electorate who are sufficiently well-organised to put pressure on the competing political parties. If, for instance, election to government requires the support of the Teamsters' Union, then any political party seeking power has to include in its programme policies which will appeal more to the Teamsters than do those of rival parties. If a group does not have the vote, there is no direct political reason why a party should take account of their interests.

Although securing the vote does not guarantee political power – far from it – disenfranchisement may be a significant disadvantage; for blacks, women and the propertyless in the past, for children today. For the majority of people the vote is a necessary, though not sufficient condition for political power.

Historically, securing the vote has been a significant goal of oppressed groups seeking emancipation. The main argument which is usually brought forward against extending the franchise is that those to whom it might be extended are either insufficiently independent, too ignorant, or too irrational to be able to make a sound judgment about what would be a sensible way to cast a vote. Because of these defects, it is not in the interests of the group concerned to have a vote, and it may lead to the unwelcome result of a government coming into power, on the strength of the votes of these people, which is not truly representative of those in the country who know what they are voting for.

This kind of argument was certainly used against extending the vote to women and blacks. In their case it now seems grossly implausible, and nobody would put forward such an argument today – except perhaps in the Republic of South Africa. With children, the argument seems to make more sense.

Children are less experienced than adults; often they are ignorant of the political issues of the day; they tend to be very influenced by the views of their parents; their grasp of political institutions is usually at best, rudimentary. To suggest that the franchise should be extended to children raises a smile. How could anyone seriously propose such a move? Why not extend the vote to babies, and to dogs, for that matter?

Well children do differ from dogs and babies at least in that only they are people. Although most children might not know much about the political system, they are able in general, to reason, and to arrive at beliefs and desires through reasoning.

This answer is, however, too swift. For not all people are competent to vote, and excluding the incompetent from the franchise is not *arbitrarily* to discriminate against them. It is not a failure to show them respect as people. Indeed to be a person requires less cognitive ability than is required in competent voting, so there is bound to be a class of people who are too young to vote, because they are too immature for political competence. We are here concerned not with all possible child-people, but only with post-10-year-olds. It could plausibly be argued that they are, by and large, incompetent to vote sensibly, mainly because of their political ignorance.

What *of* this ignorance? There is no doubt that most 10 year olds are ignorant of the subtleties of political issues of the day. However, it is not clear that this ignorance is due to limits on the possibility of psychological development. If children are developmentally capable of understanding what is going on, then it is likely that their ignorance is due to lack of education (in the broadest sense), which is in principle remediable. Anyone who seriously proposed extending the franchise to children would combine this suggestion with a plan to educate children so as to become responsible voters. Olive Stevens (1982) presents a study of the political views of several groups of 7 to 11 year old children in England, from a variety of different schools, and from various social backgrounds. Her work suggests that at least by the age of 11, children are capable of understanding key political concepts and issues. She advocates an introduction of politics into the curriculum of primary schools, in order to enable children to develop existing abilities. Of the children who entered into discussions with her she writes:

> 'they present a quite radical reappraisal of what has long been understood when people use the word "childhood"; for the children I talked to were expressing claims. What they were claiming was the proper respect, as people, of having their points of view taken seriously by others. And this they were willing to extend, to each other. Nobody laughed at anyone else's ideas; nobody said anything to diminish anyone else, or competed for attention. Their way of making their claim was to argue their own rationality, or demonstrate it by giving appropriate reasons and criteria for what they said.' (Stevens, 1982, p.175)

Of course it would be politically ridiculous to propose that from after the next election all children from 10 years upwards should have the vote. There is little evidence that many children of this age would even want the vote, or that they would know what to do with it. Any change would have to be introduced gradually – say by reducing the voting age to 17, and then seeing if there was pressure from 16 year olds to reduce it by yet another year. This process could continue until it reached the limits of development. There used to be a time when women thought it quite out of the question that they should have the vote. The very idea seemed outlandish. Indeed the early suffragette movement was ridiculed, not least of all by other women.

Children are not, on the whole, ready for the vote. The question is, should steps be taken to raise their consciousness so that more of them become so, and perhaps demand the vote? The fact that there is a good case for the present disenfranchisement of a group does not entail that it should remain permanently disfranchised. Indeed if, as for instance in South Africa, we find a society which deliberately prevents the development of political competence in a group which possesses the potential for such competence, and then goes on to deny that group the vote on the basis of its lack of competence, this is grounds for serious criticism. Ignorance and dependence are not sufficient grounds for permanently excluding a class of citizens from the vote, if something could be done to reduce the ignorance and dependence. Mill believed that participation in the political process could be an important step in fostering the development of autonomy amongst heteronomous, ignorant citizens. For this reason he thought that the vote should in his time, be extended to include the working class, who were widely regarded, not least of all by Mill himself, as ignorant enough for it to be dangerous to enable them to exercise a *decisive* influence on the election of governments. He wrote:

> 'I do not look upon equal voting as among the things which are good in themselves, provided they can be guarded against inconveniences. I look upon it as only relatively good; less objectionable than inequality of privilege grounded on irrelevant or adventitious circumstances, but in principle wrong, because recognising a wrong standard, and exercising a bad influence on the voter's mind. It is not useful, but hurtful, that the constitution of the country should declare ignorance to be entitled to as much political power as knowledge.' (Mill, 1861a, p.288)

I mention this argument not because I endorse Mill's quaint view that university lecturers should have several votes to every one of an unskilled manual worker, but because it shows that even Mill was not opposed to adults having *a* vote even though they were not ready to use it wisely.

In fact, the charge that children should be permanently disenfranchised because they lack the competence to use a vote wisely has all the hallmarks of ideological pseudo-justification. A large proportion of the electorate are ignorant of the main consequences of casting their vote one way rather than another. Yet those who oppose the enfranchisement of children do not advocate the disenfranchisement of adults who are badly informed about the issues of the day. Indeed there are moves in all liberal democracies to try to persuade ignorant and perhaps apathetic adults who do not vote, to become registered, and to exercise their 'democratic rights'.

Mill's fear of 'one person one vote' was that the working class would constitute a majority of electors under such a scheme, and would be easily seduced into electing a government which would be disastrous not only for the middle classes, but also for the workers themselves. Such a view would be unacceptable today. But even a fear such as this should not worry adults concerned about the extension of the vote to children. After all, children between 10 and 18 will most likely form quite a small minority, and they are unlikely to have huge resources at their disposal for mobilising support. Therefore it is most implausible to suggest that extending the vote to children would give ultimate power to an ignorant, incompetent section of the population. If the demands of children proved too outrageous, they could always be outvoted by adults. If children held the balance of power between two adult rival parties, then presumably, if the children's views really were outrageous, the other parties could combine to defeat them.

It is clear that moving towards the enfranchisement of children would give them, as children, a greater opportunity to exercise their autonomy, but would this benefit them overall?

There is a strong reason to suppose it would benefit their overall autonomy interests. Habits are easier to acquire when young, and harder to drop when older. If children were encouraged to take more responsibility for their lives earlier, to ask questions and seek answers, to have a legitimate interest in the affairs of government, they would be far more likely than they are at present, to develop the kind of individuality, which Mill argued in *On Liberty*, Chapter III, is a vital part of well-being. Disenfranchisement on its own is bad enough; but to keep children in a state where they are neither capable of having a sound opinion about, nor interested in, decisions which affect their lives so centrally, is a serious violation of respect for their autonomy. As things are, children have precious little opportunity to exercise their autonomy, and in particular they have no opportunity to take part in the democratic process. By the time that they are entitled to vote (18), heteronomous habits are likely to be well-entrenched. This is bad for them as children, and is likely to remain an obstacle to their autonomy throughout adulthood.

But people do not have only autonomy interests. They have mental state interests as well. If a person, making an autonomous decision, is likely to do herself great harm, respect for her may justify the undermining of the decision. For respect requires that concern be shown for *all* the vital interests of the person respected. Is it plausible to claim that to move towards the enfranchisement of children would work against their mental state interests to such an extent as to outweigh the obvious gains to their autonomy interests of enfranchisement? I think not.

The crucial factor here is time. The fear would be that if children had the vote they would be exclusively concerned for their immediate, or at least very near, well-being, at the expense of their lives as a whole. Perhaps the main reason for this is that children have different time horizons from adults. For a 10 year old a year is an awful long time (a tenth of his already-experienced life), and life beyond that time might appear to a child to be beyond the horizon of his concerns. Even if children could not form a government, they might be able to exercise sufficient influence on the major political parties that at least some of their proposals would be accepted by any party forming a government. Such policies, although appealing to children, whilst they were children, might have long-term deleterious effects. It is sometimes said that children would vote to abolish paternalistic legislation which genuinely serves their long-term interests. For example, they might seek to abolish compulsory schooling, repeal protective industrial legislation, and perhaps act in ways which would bring about the end of civilisation as we know it.

In answer to these charges it could be said, first, that much of the existing paternalistic legislation is *not* obviously in the best interests of children, particularly when account is taken of their autonomy interests; and where such legislation is necessary now, this may be because insufficient attention has been paid in the past to the development of children's autonomy. Second, it is also not clear that children *would* support more imprudent policies than do others. Governments typically pursue short-term strategies which are aimed at sustaining them in power by appealing to the short-term interests of an ill-informed electorate of adults, who were never granted the chance to develop their autonomy as children.

As things stand, it is clear that the interests of children, particularly their autonomy interests, are not given proper weight by the political system. One of the main reasons for people seeking enfranchisement is that others cannot be relied upon either to seek to promote the interests of the disfranchised, or, even if they seek it, to know it as well as those on whose behalf they would be acting. I am sure this is true of all groups in society. However there is a special reason why adults might not be especially concerned to introduce legislation which is in the interests of children. Although it is true that all adults *were* once children, they will never be children again, so what happens to children as a result of their policies will only be of indirect concern to them. On the other hand, policies affecting older people will directly affect children, so they have a direct stake in promoting the welfare of older people. Of course this effect is partly offset because many adults have children about whose welfare they are deeply concerned; and even the childless may desire to promote the interests of the young. But this factor should not completely be ignored.

It could be argued that disenfranchising the young is, unlike disenfranchisement on grounds of sex or skin colour, not unfairly discriminatory because, whereas the young may expect to become enfranchised when they reach the age of majority, women do not expect to become men, nor is there a time at which people may expect to change skin colour. The restriction on children does not discriminate against any people throughout their whole lives. All people were children once, and may expect to become adults some time.

This argument is superficially attractive, but I think in the end it is unconvincing. Consider an analogous argument for disenfranchising the old. As people grow old their perspective on the world changes, and they become increasingly unable to comprehend changes which are taking place in their own country and the world. Consequently their opinions are worth less than those of people in the middle period of their lives. Excluding the elderly from the vote would greatly reduce the influence of outdated and irrelevant opinions on the decision-making process. Those reaching the age of disenfranchisement, say 65, would have no reason to complain, for they will have had some 47 years with the vote. This is uncompelling, but what *is* wrong with the argument for disenfranchising the elderly?

First, even if it is true that the elderly on the whole, represent outdated views, it does not follow that they are incompetent to express a genuine opinion. And the Kantian principle does not state that respect should be shown only to people who are particularly well-informed, or in fact *do* make good decisions. If the vote were extended only to those who could at the time make wise, well-informed choices, the franchise would be very small; and this would be inconsistent with the principles of liberal democracy.

Second, although, as I have said, it is in the interests of the young to have policies which will benefit the elderly (that is benefit those who will become elderly), people are very often not prudent. Unless elderly people have the vote, there is little chance that politicians will promote their interests. Any political party needs widespread support among the elderly if it is to be elected; so there is some pressure on each party to include programmes which will appeal to the elderly.

If at the age of 65 people were suddenly disenfranchised, it would be as if to say to them: 'You are no longer worthy of inclusion within the scope of the Kantian principle of respect for people'. And yet there is no reason to suppose that people over this age cease to be people, or worthy of respect.

The principle of respect is not only neutral in regard to different people, but it should apply neutrally across time. If the argument for excluding the old from the political process fails, then so should the argument for excluding the young.

Liberals who believe in respect for autonomy face a dilemma.

If they are to defend themselves against the thoroughgoing elitist who claims that only the super-intelligent and well-informed should have the vote – to ensure that only the best governments are elected, they need to rely on an argument which supports not the status-quo, but moving towards an extension of the franchise to children. According to Mill:

> 'any education which aims at making human beings other than machines, in the long run makes them claim to have control over their own lives.' (Mill, 1861a, p.207)

The drift of the argument of this section is that if children demand the vote, then respect for them, particularly if one takes autonomy seriously, should lead towards their enfranchisement. Of course not many children do want the vote now. A genuine respect for them would generate educational (in the broadest sense) programmes which would lead them to want control over their own lives sooner rather than later. The desire to vote would stem from a more general desire for self-determination. Respect for children at least gives us a strong reason to put such a programme to the test.

Let us now turn to a discussion of education to see whether present practice is consistent with prevalent principle.

Education

It is common practice for children to be compelled to attend school from the age of 5 until 16. As we saw earlier, it seems that much of the impetus for compulsory schooling has come not primarily from a concern for the educational interests of the children, but for other social reasons, such as clearing the streets from actual or potential trouble makers, and easing pressures of various sorts on the job market. But can compulsory schooling be justified by concern for the children whose liberty is restricted? In particular, are present educational practices consistent with a respect for the autonomy of children?

If 10 year olds are developmentally capable of expressing a genuine preference for one political party over another, 5 year olds are certainly able to have and express preferences about

whether or not to attend school. Many parents will be familiar
with the problem of having to cajole and possibly coerce their 5
year old to attend the first day at school. Throughout their school
career, right up to the age of 16 a large number of children go to
school primarily because non-attendance is accompanied with
severe sanctions.

Once again, the liberal who cares about autonomy is faced with
a dilemma. How is it possible to justify compulsory schooling for
children who are people, without justifying the most appalling
paternalistic restrictions on adults? If, as a matter of principle, it
is wrong to act paternalistically towards reasonably incompetent
adults, on the grounds that respect should be shown for their
liberty no less than for that of the more competent, is it not
unfair to act paternalistically towards children, who may be no
less, and possibly more competent than these adults? Let us recall
Mill's Liberty Principle which states that a person:

'cannot rightfully be compelled to do or forbear because it will
be better for him to do so, because it will make him happier,
because in the opinion of others, to do so would be wise, or
even right.' (Mill, 1859, p.73)

In order to begin to answer this puzzle posed by the attraction
of both the principle of respect for people, and the view that the
interests of children justify compulsory education, one needs to
return to a consideration of autonomy. People have two sorts of
interests – mental state interests, and autonomy interests. One of
the special attractions of liberal theory is its recognition of the
independent weight of autonomy interests. It differs from
Benthamite utilitarianism because it recognises that people have
interests which go beyond living a pleasant, pain-free existence.
Paternalistic restrictions on liberty, which are apparently justified
by appeal to the pleasant mental states they might promote, or
unpleasant ones they might avoid, are often unwarranted, because
they constitute a serious violation of their subject's autonomy
interests. If, as has been argued, it is not plausible to treat the
non-infringement of autonomy as a moral constraint, then in
principle, restrictions on individuals' liberty which promote a
person's overall autonomy interests can be justified. This is, in
fact, a popular justification for compulsory schooling.

In so far as the appeal to autonomy is taken seriously, compulsory schooling should be judged according to whether or not it promotes the overall autonomy interests of children through time. In particular it may be justifiable, out of concern for a person's autonomy interests to prevent him from exercising a choice on a particular occasion if this is necessary for enabling him to develop his capacity to make more autonomous choices later. It is very likely that ensuring a 5 year old goes to school, even if compulsion is necessary, promotes the child's autonomy interests (assuming the school isn't unusually awful), since it helps the child to be weaned off dependency on his parents, and ensures that he will be subject to new stimuli, and therefore become more capable of determining his own life. However, as children grow older, such claims become decreasingly plausible. Although I would not wish to base a general argument about the efficacy of a practice on a single example, I do think it is worth considering this quotation from a very articulate 17 year old, describing why he abandoned his intention to become a school teacher:

'It occurred to me to probe my memory and find my 11th, 12th, 13th and 14th years, though not so long ago, but like so many things, easily forgotten. I remember particularly that I had a mind of my own, then, and a will to choose. I had like many others, preferences, which were denied me. I did not like P.E., but I was made to do P.E. I did not like to sit still, but I was made to sit still. Then it occurred to me that to be a teacher I would have to comply with the rules of that tyrannical and degenerate system of adult over child despotism. No matter how kind I would wish to be to the pupils, I would have to comply with the base rules, and, what is worse, I would have to impose the rules upon living, thinking and active human beings. Not only would this completely demoralise me but it would make me feel hopelessly hypocritical, and I would have to make "people" do things they did not want to do, such as sitting still. Thus with the development of my adopted philosophy, I have had to turn my back on that noble profession.' (Bristow, 1979, pp.176–7)

Although life in school is not uniformly as grim as the above quotation suggests, and one can find people who look back on their school days with pleasure and appreciation, the reality of much secondary education is that pupils' autonomy interests are not served well. It is no doubt true that being made to sit still and quietly through lessons you do not want to attend, on subjects in which you have little or no interest, is a good training for a sort of self-discipline. But an educational system which was geared to promote widespread autonomy amongst its pupils would provide an environment which stimulated critical self-awareness, a desire to question received wisdom, and self-directedness; and most schools are unable to provide this.

This failure is not so much a failure of individual teachers, as a structural inevitability. The chronic lack of resources for state education means that most children spend most of their school days in classes of about 30, where it is simply not possible to encourage individual initiative on a scale which would be required by a genuine effort to promote autonomy. With such large classes consisting of many children who do not wish to be there, the teacher is often forced into the role of jailer. Her first priority is to ensure that there is discipline – imposed discipline; quiet, if not peace. It is, for many teachers, just physically impossible to give children the time and space needed for developing a high level of autonomy. Resources are allocated so that younger children each receive less resources than older, and abler students receive more than the less able. It might be instructive to compare the resources available for children in a working class comprehensive school with those which undergraduates at Oxford enjoy, being taught in classes of one or two, many lectures to choose from on a wide range of subjects, and excellent libraries and equipment. Personal development is greatly helped by personal attention. It is a pity that very often those who are most in need of personal tuition are among the least likely to receive it. An educational system which genuinely sought to promote autonomy neutrally among those going through it would look quite different from present systems. It would have a structure which positively encouraged people to challenge received wisdoms – not just to accept views, but to accept or reject them on the basis of having understood the reasons for them.

To say that educational systems work to maintain the stability of the society in which they function is almost platitudinous. A corollary of this is that a society's educational system provides a pretty good picture of the broader structure of the society. In the United Kingdom, and I dare say other liberal democracies, the liberty of children is greatly restricted. Given the fact that the economies of these societies require large numbers of people to spend their lives doing work which is menial, unstimulating and intrinsically boring, whilst a minority thrive on profits made from the fruits of these people's labour, it is not surprising that most children's autonomy is not properly promoted. This is put rather eleoquently by the famous advocate of free schools, A. S. Neill, in an essay he wrote when 87 years old (a testament to the view that not all old people have only old-fashioned ideas):

> 'If all kids were brought up in freedom . . . you wouldn't have a sick world, an aggressive world . . . People would not allow their lives to be controlled so much by other people. The reason why workers in Britain never strike for workers' control [he should have said "hardly ever"] is that they have been educated to be inferior, to stay in their own lower class, to take orders. It is an education for submission to the *status quo*, an education for despair. Kids who had been used to participating in a direct democracy (not a fake representative democracy) from the word go, would not grow up to suffer from apathy, alienation, and blind submission to authority with inner hatred and self-hatred as the other side of the coin.' (Neill, 1972, p.159)

These sentiments may appear naively optimistic about human nature. But they should be taken seriously by liberals who believe that respect should be shown for the individual. It does look as if the justifications for the present compulsory education system are rationalisations, part of an ideology. It looks as if the present socio-economic system in liberal democracies requires a majority of the population to be unconfident, apathetic, compliant, un-self-reliant. For few people whose intelligence and individuality had been anywhere near fully developed would be willing to work (or be unemployed) in the circumstances which are the lot of perhaps most. We have here a case where there is a structural necessity for a certain type of education system. This system is justified on the grounds that it best serves the interests of those who pass through it. It appears that the system does not, in fact, do this. The most plausible conclusion is that the system really benefits only a minority of the population, and that the justifications offered are ideological.

It does not, incidentally, follow from this, that, in the interests of children's autonomy, school should suddenly become optional. Of course it would be an excellent goal to aim for schools which were so attractive to children that they wanted to go to them without threats; but this is at best a long-term goal. In the absence of such a radical change, a real problem is that those who do worst out of the present educational system as it is, would probably drop out of the school system altogether. Evidence is conflicting about whether or not this would benefit these children, or be disastrous for them. On the one hand, they might be forced into exceptionally exploitative labour at a very tender age (school can offer at least a temporary reprieve from this). On the other hand many children may learn more 'on the street', than as unwilling participants in school.

I think that, as with the exclusion of children from the vote, it is misleading to base the case for maintaining the *status quo* on imagining what would happen if suddenly children were no longer compelled to go to school. The point is that there is no significant movement towards trying to create an environment where children would want to go to school; just as there is no attempt to educate children to become interested in the political process, in seeking to control their own lives. Michael Duane (1972), a progressive headmaster whose state school was eventually closed down by the local authority, again optimistically, describes his vision of an acceptable school system:

'The school of the future, while it may have certain superficial resemblances to schools that we see today, will differ in the most fundamental point that the children will be free to choose whether or not to come to school and what they shall do while they are there. Most people when presented with such a prospect immediately assume that no children will want to attend school, or that, if they do, there will be bedlam of such a kind that teachers will be unable to teach. In fact, as can be seen in the few schools where such conditions prevail, not only is there regular attendance at lessons, but the actual discipline or rather self-discipline within the class is of a higher order.

The function of the teacher changes from that of stuffing knowledge into the child, whether he likes it or not, to that of being at hand as an experienced advisor in providing the technical skills and knowledge that will enable the child to achieve his aims. The teacher will, in fact, be rather more deeply occupied in assembling the most educative materials and problems to suit the individual children in his care than in simply pressing them to go through a routine of learning designed for mass teaching.' (Duane, 1972, pp.256–7)

The problem, as visionaries such as Neill and Duane no doubt discovered, is that it has not proved possible to educate the masses to become autonomous in a class-divided society. They describe the sort of education that would be fitting for the liberal democratic belief in respect for people, but sadly it has remained available only for a privileged few.

Conclusion

Our consideration of the franchise and education suggests that, at least in these areas, the autonomy of children is not seriously promoted. In so far as they are *capable* of exercising autonomous choice, they are denied the *opportunity* to do so; and their potential for becoming more autonomous remains largely undeveloped. This is indefensible unless the neglect of children's autonomy is essential for the vital interests of children, or the majority of the population, and there is no reason to suppose that it is. The problem for liberals is that some values which lie at the heart of liberalism are, in their implications, radical. It may well be that the values cannot be instantiated in a class-divided society, with widespread economic and political inequality, and deep conflicts of interests. And yet liberal theory has in practice been precisely a theory for such societies. At least as far as children are concerned, it seems to be true that liberal democratic society is unable to deliver what its own principles declare to be essential.

In the next chapter we shall discuss another group of people who are normally excluded from anti-paternalist liberty principles – the mentally disordered.

9 Mental Disorder

'The aim of psychiatry is to promote health and personal growth . . . Every patient must be offered the best therapy available and be treated with the solicitude and respect due to the dignity of all human beings and to their autonomy over their lives and health.' (From The Declaration of Hawaii, adopted by the General Assembly of the World Psychiatric Association, Honolulu, 1977).

As I have stressed, respect for the individual, and particularly a belief in the vital importance of personal autonomy, are key values in the justification of liberal democracy. As a general rule people should be allowed to run their own lives, and make their own mistakes, provided that by so doing they do not interfere with others' opportunities to do the same. We have just considered one exception to this principle – children. There is another notable exception – the mentally disordered.

There are two broad categories of mental disorder, into which the various specific disorders fall. The first may be called 'mental handicap', the other 'mental illness'. My main concern in this chapter will be with mental illness, but I shall begin by saying a little about 'mental handicap'.

Mental handicap

Handicaps may or may not be curable. They are disabilities which make it harder for their bearer to function as effectively as 'normal' people. Thus, to be born with a withered arm is to have a handicap. We have, I think, a fairly clear idea of physical handicap. But what is mental handicap? According to Tony Whitehead:

'Mental handicap is a term now used to describe what used to be referred to as mental subnormality, and before that, as mental deficiency. Mental handicap, in essence, is a disorder of intelligence, which has been described by W. Stern as "the general ability to adapt to new situations by means of purposeful thinking".' (Whitehead, 1982, p.5)

Mentally handicapped people, then, have a below average competence to adapt to new situations. They may be unable to understand what their legal obligations are, and they may be especially gullible, being, as it were, easily led astray. However, as the definition of 'intelligence' is controversial, controversy will always surround the concept of 'mental handicap'. Furthermore, the fact that intelligence is a matter of degree, rather than an all or none phenomenon, means that restrictions on the freedom of mentally handicapped people to live their lives (perhaps unwisely) as they choose, raise difficult ethical issues. These ethical issues are most pressing, not in regard to the severely handicapped, who are incapable even of survival without paternalistic assistance, but with those whom Daniel Wikler (1979) calls 'the mildly retarded':

'In many states, the mildly retarded must submit to the guidance of competent persons or authorities before making important decisions. These include the decision to marry, to have children, to enter into financial contracts, and to live alone. Generally speaking, adults of normal intelligence may make these decisions without obtaining the consent of anyone, and they value this autonomy.' (Wikler, 1979, p.377)

There is an interesting analogy here between the mentally handicapped and children. It is obvious that very young children need control, just in order to survive. For they lack an understanding of danger, and the basic ability to look after themselves. The same is true of the severely mentally handicapped whether they are young or old. On the other hand older children, say adolescents, do have a *basic* understanding of how to take care of themselves, and they may have strong preferences about how to live their lives. Similarly, the mildly retarded have these basic competences.

Wikler presents a powerful challenge to our existing paternalistic policies towards the mildly retarded. The challenge comes from considering the fact that the abilities which are relevant to the categorisation of individuals as mentally handicapped are a matter of degree. It is not that there is a significant difference between all mentally handicapped people and everyone else. In so far as it may be necessary, legally, to have some (arbitrary) cut-off point separating those who are to be subject to paternalistic control from the rest, it could be argued that the present point includes too many as in need of too much control. Many mentally handicapped people are denied the chance to exercise what autonomy they have.

Wikler's argument is that the paternalistic restrictions we impose on the mildly retarded are, although possibly motivated by benevolence, unfair. The usual ground for such restrictions is that the retarded are not as well able to look after themselves, and make wise choices, as are the 'normal', and that the 'normal' could better protect the interests of the 'subnormal' than they can themselves. If this is acceptable, then why not adopt the general principle that those of superior intelligence should impose paternalistic restrictions on the merely normal? If the grounds for the restrictions on the mildly retarded are that others could make better choices for them, such restrictions could, in principle, justifiably be extended to cover most of the population. Few who accept present practices would approve of this.

It appears that the mildly mentally handicapped are denied the protection of the Kantian principle, even though they are undoubtedly persons, and thus should be covered by it. They and adolescents both have desires to live their own lives, which are particularly disregarded by present paternalistic practices. Scant consideration is given to their autonomy. For although they are less autonomous than most adults, they lack neither the capacity nor the desire to make their own important life-affecting choices. Yet these autonomy interests are, to a large extent, sacrificed – for what? At the moment society is organised so that mentally handicapped people are in serious danger of entering into disadvantageous financial contracts, and being exploited by others. Laws which restrict the freedom of the mentally handicapped protect them against such exploitations. No doubt, given the way present society is organised, there is a good case for these protections. However, as Wikler points out, the standards for competence and incompetence are *set* by society, and could change if social practices changed. It is clear that present society is not organised for the benefit of the mentally handicapped. How could it be so?

> 'Society might have instituted rules allowing persons to annul contracts if they proved inconvenient or if the contractor misjudged his resources at the time of bargaining. Similarly, the burden of a decision to procreate would have been lighter had custom not assigned to parents the responsibility for caring for their offspring. Under these conditions, persons whose mental powers are much weaker than the average would be competent to enter contracts, marry, and make otherwise important decisions without regularly risking serious reverses which they could not predict and understand. The threshold of competence and mental impairment would be set that much lower.' (Ibid., p.387)

Why is society not so organised? Wikler's answer is that such arrangements would be worse for normal people, since, for example, it might put an end to trade which was not conducted through cash transactions. Wikler is right to point out that in one sense, society could change so as to give more weight to the needs for self-determination of the mentally handicapped, and that whether it should or not is a question of distributive justice – of, as he puts it, 'distributing the burdens of incompetence'.

Wikler argues that there is a straightforward conflict between the autonomy interests of the mildly retarded, and the convenience of the majority. If it is more important to protect the vital interests of all than to promote the less-than-vital interests of some, then the standards of competence for most transactions should be lowered. Whilst I agree with this, I have been persuaded by John Baker in correspondence, that Wikler both underestimates the problems of generally lowering standards of competence, and exaggerates the conflict between the interests of the mildly retarded and the 'normal' majority. If the changes to contract law, mentioned above, were introduced, the freedom of the 'normal' would be greatly reduced. The freedom which is presently denied the mentally handicapped is precisely a freedom to enter genuine contracts, to marry and so on. A society with

Wikler's proposed changes would deny this freedom to everyone, since people would only be able to 'Wikler contract' and 'Wikler marry'. What is crucially wrong with the present structure of contracts is not the structure itself, but rather the absence of alternative structures for people other than the 'normal', in particular the mentally handicapped. One possibility would be that the mildly retarded could carry a 'handicap card', analogous to a physically disabled person's card, which, for example, entitled them to refunds for unwise purchases, and for the easy annulment of disadvantageous contracts. Admittedly this would restrict the liberty of the mentally handicapped *somewhat*, and there would have to be strong safeguards against abuse, but it would afford the mildly retarded greater opportunities to determine their own lives.

These sorts of changes *could* be introduced with comparatively little cost within liberal democratic societies – bringing about an enormous gain in autonomy for many mentally handicapped people. But such a move is not on the political agenda, and this is indicative of a lack of concern for the autonomy of the mentally handicapped.

A rigid classification of people into the mentally handicapped and the rest is an ideological confusion. Present paternalistic restrictions on the conduct of the mildly handicapped, although ostensibly designed to benefit them, do not take seriously their interests in autonomy. Arrangements could be made much better to promote the vital interests in autonomy of the mentally handicapped without injuring the vital interests of others, or indeed the mental state interests of the handicapped themselves. Since in any event the autonomy of the mentally handicapped is impaired, social justice requires that such arrangements be made. This would enable the mentally handicapped to develop and enjoy the benefits of such autonomy as they were capable of, and seems to be required by the Kantian principle of respect.

Once again, it appears that the practices of liberal democratic societies do not accord with their principles of equal respect for people, and the supreme importance to be attached to individual self-development and self-determination. Moral principles and practice are in deep, possibly fundamental conflict.

Mental illness

The 1959 Mental Health Act (amended 1983) was the last of a series of major reforms in Britain, which, starting in the late eighteenth century, has transformed insanity into a medical problem. Given the horrific way in which mentally disturbed people have been treated in the past, these changes were widely welcomed. The Mental Health Act firmly established the principle that 'mentally ill' people could receive treatment on the National Health Service in the same way as other 'informal' patients. Recognising that they were ill, they would seek the help of the medical profession, who would attempt to cure the ailment. There is no shame in going into hospital to have an appendectomy; nor is there in having regular insulin injections to control diabetes. Similarly there should be no shame in going into hospital for electro-convulsive therapy to cure a depression; nor in being on a course of phenothiazine injections to control schizophrenia. And yet . . . and yet there are huge differences. Some notable writers, for example Thomas Szasz (1961) have denied that mental illnesses exist at all, and Szasz (1971) argued that the claim that there are functional mental illnesses is an ideological confusion, used to oppress scapegoats in the way that the ideology of witchcraft oppressed unfortunate people of earlier generations. Furthermore, a substantial number of mental patients in hospitals are compulsory patients (16 per cent in England and Wales, a far higher proportion in the United States). Forcing people to stay in hospital and have treatment is a serious restriction of their liberty. How can present practices be reconciled with a respect for autonomy? Are the 'mentally ill' unfairly treated? Is their autonomy unjustifiably curtailed? Does labelling people as 'mentally ill' in itself undermine their autonomy, by treating a rational response to a hostile situation as a 'condition' to be treated?

Illness

The so-called 'anti-psychiatry' lobby, of which Szasz is the best-known member, claim that whereas there are genuine physical illnesses, with objective symptoms (a syndrome), caused by biological abnormalities, what is called 'mental illness' is an invented myth. Of course there are organic diseases of the brain (such as tumours) which cause people to behave in bizarre ways, but 'schizophrenia', 'depression' and 'mania' for example, as purely 'functional diseases', are inventions rather than discoveries. To attach these labels to patients is a way to avoid treating them with the respect due to people – as ends in themselves. If a citizen is depressed, or finds she is not coping adequately with her life, and she wishes to consult a specialist, such as a psychiatrist or psychotherapist, she should of course be allowed to, but only as the result of an agreed private contract. On the other hand, if she breaks the law on account of a so-called 'mental illness', she should be punished, just like anyone else. She should take the consequences of her actions. To deny this to a person is to fail to give proper weight to her autonomy.

There are two distinct questions here, which may be confused. The first concerns the appropriateness of regarding as illnesses those mentally distressing states, which are referred to as 'schizophrenia', 'depression' and so on; the other is about the treatment of people in such states. I shall discuss them in turn.

Much of the anti-psychiatry argument about the non-reality of 'mental illness' rests on the claim that attributions of 'mental illness' are relative to value judgments about acceptable attitudes and conduct. In Ken Kesey's novel *One Flew Over the Cuckoo's Nest* the hero, Randall MacMurphy, is a larger-than-life rebel, who challenges the powers of established authority first within the armed forces, and then in a mental hospital. He refuses to accept the restrictive rules of the institutions in which he finds himself, is diagnosed as mentally ill, and ends up a vegetable, the victim of a frontal lobotomy performed against his will.

It is unquestionably true that there have been cases of people being diagnosed as mentally ill without evidence that they are genuinely ill. This diagnosis could then be used to legitimise incarceration or character-affecting treatment, ostensibly in the patient's real interests. In the past (and some would argue, even today) many people have been labelled 'mentally ill' just because they behaved in a socially unacceptable way. A notorious example, discussed by Szasz (1971), is 'masturbatory insanity', described by a well-known nineteenth-century expert in the following terms. Among the disturbances associated with (male) masturbation are:

'Melancholia, stuporous insanity, katatonia, and insanity of pubescence . . . The ordinary characteristics of the masturbator are, however, found in addition. Thus such lunatics are usually retired, sly, suspicious, hypochondriacal, indolent, mean, and cowardly. They are capital simulators, and develop an art in concealing and in practising their vice which is in remarkable contrast with their stupidity, apathy, and feeble-mindedness in other respects. The prognosis of the psychoses associated with masturbation in males is bad. A variety of primary deterioration marked by moral perversion is observed in young victims of the habit, which yields to treatment if the habit is abolished.' (Spitzka, 1883, pp.378–80) [Quoted in Szasz, 1971, p.218]

It does not, however, follow that mental illness *is* a myth. Admittedly there is a potential for psychiatry to be used as a force for imposing conformity to societal norms upon people. But even mainstream psychiatrists regard the use of psychiatry for overt or covert political purposes as an abuse, and they would certainly join in roundly condemning the Victorian attitude to and treatment of masturbation.

Nevertheless, it is hard to deny that ascriptions of mental illness rest on value judgments – about what are desirable and undesirable attitudes and conduct. The main mistake made by the anti-psychiatry lobby is not to recognise that ascriptions of *physical* as well as mental illness and diseases rest on value judgments. This point is made most eloquently by Peter Sedgwick (1982). He was a strong and forceful critic of anti-psychiatry, whilst by no means a member of the medical establishment. Of illness he writes:

'To complain of illness, or to ascribe illness to another person, is not to make a descriptive statement about physiology or anatomy. Concepts of illness were in use among people for centuries before the advent of any reliable knowledge of the human body, and are still employed today within societies which favour a non-physiological (magical or religious) account of the nature of human maladies.' (Sedgwick, 1982, p.32)

The fact that illness-ascription employs value judgments should not cause very severe anxiety. It does not mean, for instance, that the criteria for being ill are purely arbitrary. What then, are the criteria for the ascription of illness? First illness is a kind of disfavoured deviancy from an expected norm. (Geniuses are not automatically regarded as ill, though they are exceptional). Second, an illness is a recognisable syndrome – a recognisable pattern of symptoms. Third, there is the supposition that the symptoms have causes which can be explained by experts (doctors, witch-doctors, shamans etc.), who usually also have prime responsibility for treatment.

To be ill is to have something wrong with you – to have a condition which is harmful. Controversy about whether or not a person is ill may well be related to disputes about whether or not a certain condition is harmful. There will be agreement over the vast majority of cases. We mainly associate disputes about whether or not a person is ill with attributions of *mental* disorder; but there can be similar disputes about the physical. Wing (1978) mentions Dubos's (1965) description of:

> 'A South American tribe in which a disfiguring disease, dyschromic spirochaetosis, characterised by multicoloured spots on the skin, was so common that those who did *not* have it were regarded as abnormal and excluded from marriage. Dyschromic spirochaetosis is a serious disease, recognisable at once to any expert, but only those who had it were thought to be healthy.' (Wing, 1978, p.15)

In so far as all we mean by an illness is something like that outlined above, there's nothing wrong with talking about *mental* illnesses, and it does serve a purpose. The claim that there cannot be mental illness rests on the false assumption that being ill requires one to have a specific 'illness', such illnesses all forming natural kinds with specific physical organic causes – rather in the way that smallpox was caused by a virus. Of course there is no equivalent of the smallpox virus in such complicated affective and behavioural disturbances as 'depression', 'mania' and 'schizophrenia', and our diagnostic categories may come to be regarded as primitive (see Sedgwick, 1982, p.38). However, it does not follow that there are no mental illnesses in the sense outlined above.

Furthermore, this model does not commit one to what Sedgwick calls the 'technologising of illness'. Some people fear that conceding the possibility of mental illness commits one to accepting the so-called 'medical model' of mental illness. Perhaps followers of this model tend to concentrate too much on drug therapies, which are directed just at symptom removal. It is important to distinguish criticism of the treatment of mental illness from claims that mental illness is a myth. Ill people may be simply regarded as malfunctioning machines who may be put right by medical practitioners in the same sort of way as a car may be fixed at a garage. To suggest that depression could, like a fast-idling car, be cured by a quick service may be dehumanising for the depressed person with genuine social problems. But so, when one thinks about it, can be the technological treatment of the symptoms of various physical ailments. Perhaps the professional dominance of doctors (see Freidson, 1970) should be challenged. To go the way of the anti-psychiatry lobby is, however, at once to concede too much to those who do not respect the autonomy of patients who are physically ill, whilst denying the legitimacy of essential health care for those who suffer from mental distress.

I believe that the most important and pervasive feature of mental *handicap* is the loss of autonomy which this condition constitutes – the lack of control over one's life, autonomy being a primary good, heretonomy an ill. Mental *illness* is more complicated, since within much mental illness there is not only loss of autonomy, but also severe pain. As the relief of pain (in which people have a vital interest) may conflict with the promotion of a mentally ill person's autonomy, there will be cases of mental illness where it is quite legitimate not to regard the patient's autonomy as paramount. On the other hand, much mental illness is characterised by the patient losing autonomy – either through being deluded, or through losing the capacity to order her affective states. To the extent that loss of autonomy is the problem, then restoration of autonomy should be a key criterion by which one should judge supposed treatments, and it is to a discussion of treatments that I now turn.

Treatment

It would be quite inappropriate in a work of this kind to go into great detail about treatments of mental disorders. So I shall restrict myself to remarks which, though general, are I hope, not too general to support my argument about how the principle of respect for the individual is, and should be applied to mental patients in liberal democratic society.

The most obvious threat to the autonomy of mental patients comes from the fact that it is possible for people to be committed to mental hospitals involuntarily, and to receive treatment against their will. In its very nature compulsion violates an individual's interest in the exercise of autonomy. It does not, however, automatically follow that the use of compulsion in the treatment of mental illness is unjustifiable on the grounds that it cannot be reconciled with a proper regard for individual autonomy.

As was argued in Chapter 6, the Kantian principle of respect for persons, from which is derived the injunction not to violate individual autonomy, should not be taken as imposing a moral constraint upon action. For it is possible that the substantive aim behind the principle will sometimes be best served by thwarting a person's desires at a particular time. Whether or not compulsory hospitalisation and treatment of mental patients are justifiable on these grounds is a case in point – it is a genuine question – rather in the way in which it is a genuine question whether or not the autonomy of children is best promoted by compelling unwilling children to attend school.

There are three direct grounds for restricting an individual's liberty. These are, where restriction is in the individual's overall autonomy interests; second, where non-restriction would cause a more serious violation of the individual's mental state interests; and finally, where non-interference would harm the interests of a third party.

Law-makers in liberal democratic states have sought, especially in the last thirty years, to strike a balance between respect for these possibly conflicting interests. If there were no compulsory treatment of mental illness, some people who, as things stand, greatly benefit from treatment (in respect of either their autonomy or mental state interests) would be worse off; and other people's safety might be threatened by the conduct of the deranged. On the other hand, there is a danger that laws may allow for the unjustified detention of people who are merely deviant – who do not share popular values, or who are critical of the prevalent political institutions (see Bloch, 1981).

There has been a marked shift during the twentieth century, in attitudes towards hospitalisation of the mentally ill. Whereas in late nineteenth-century England, only about 8 per cent of those in mental institutions were deemed curable, nowadays mental patients tend to be in hospital for only short periods of treatment. This is reflected in the legislation governing compulsory admission to hospital. There is a provision for emergency admission for a maximum of three days, during which time a proper assessment can be made. Many of the 7000 or so compulsory detainees in England and Wales are in hospital under section 25 of the Mental Health Act. This allows for 28 days' detention, and applications to detain a person under this section may be made by a specially qualified social worker or the patient's nearest relative, on the grounds:

'(a) that he is suffering from mental disorder of a nature or degree which warrants the detention of the patient in a hospital under observation (assessment) [with or without medical treatment] for at least a limited period; and
(b) that he ought to be so detained in the interests of his own health or safety or with a view to the protection of other persons.' (Whitehead, 1982, p.62)

These orders require the signature of two doctors.

The majority of inmates in mental hospitals in Britain are short-stay ('acute') patients. Acute patients enter hospital in a crisis, which is handled by the hospital. In the majority of cases the crisis is over within a month, and the patient is restored to the community, probably continuing with out-patient care and medication. This approach certainly reduces the debilitating effects upon patients which can befall anyone who spends a protracted period in what Erving Goffman (1961) described as a 'total institution'. Patients are at least encouraged to regain sufficient autonomy to be able to survive outside the institution. This is in stark contrast to the asylum described by a writer in the *Edinburgh Review* of 1870, which was:

'very well suited to a workhouse, but totally unfitted to an asylum for mental cure. Individuality is entirely overlooked; indeed the whole of asylum life is the opposite of the ordinary mode of living of the working classes. When the visitor strolls along the galleries filled with listless patients, the utter absence of any object to afford amusement or occupation strikes him most painfully. It is remarked with infinite approval now and then by the Commissioners that the walls have been enlivened with some cheap paper, that a few prints have been hung in the galleries, that a fernery has been established – matters all very well in their way, but utterly inadequate to take the place of the moving sights of the outside world.' (Edinburgh Review, 1870, p.223, quoted in Scull, 1979, p.199)

Andrew Scull in his seminal work (1979) on the social organisation of insanity in nineteenth-century England presented a convincing case for the claim that the growth of the big asylums throughout the century, and the medical professionalisation of mental health care did not primarily serve the interests of the patients, and was a response to other social pressures, notably the growth in the unemployable poor. In recent years there has been a move towards reducing the proportion of patients in mental institutions. Indeed, between 1954 and 1971 the number of beds occupied by mental patients in England and Wales dropped from 354 per 100000 population to 225 per 100000 (Wing, 1978, p.137), at a time when those suffering from mental disorders was actually increasing.

These changes have come about as a result of the 1962 Hospital Plan which sought to replace the traditional large asylums with alternative forms of care, which would enable the mentally ill to receive more personal attention, affording greater respect for their autonomy. It is clear that reducing coercion and hospitalisation is *prima facie* a step in this direction.

The vision which is shared by many supporters of the Hospital Plan is for mentally ill people to be, wherever possible, able to live in their communities, cared for primarily by family and friends, with effective backup being provided by social and medical services. It would give mentally ill people and their families greater control over their lives, and thus promote their autonomy interests in addition to other welfare interests.

The move towards shifting the care of the mentally disordered away from mental hospitals back into the community is strong not just in Britain, but also in North America and the countries of Western Europe. The main official justification for such a move *is* that it offers a better chance for mental patients to realise their autonomy – to have more control over their own lives. But removal from, or denial of access to, mental hospitals is not, by itself, sufficient for this purpose.

At the very least there is a need to offer suitable alternative facilities to cover the useful functions of asylum, shelter, supervision and basic nursing, which have traditionally been offered by mental hospitals, however inadequately. Unfortunately, to provide satisfactory community resources would be expensive, and it is not clear that the extra facilities have been, or are likely to be, provided. Wing outlines what he thinks would be required as follows:

'This means the provision of well-staffed units for demented old people, at a time when the ordinary hospital facilities for geriatric medicine are seriously deficient. It means the provision of a wide range of protected environments, including hostels, group homes, and subsidised housing. It means the provision of "secure" accommodation other than in mental hospitals. It means the provision of extra units with special facilities for physically handicapped people who are mentally ill. Many of these extra services are supposed to be provided by local government social service departments, rather than by hospital authorities, but the current financial climate is not favourable.' (p.203)

In the preceding chapter I argued that paternalistic restrictions on the liberty of children are supported by ideological reasoning in so far as the supposed justifications for the policies provide a smokescreen for what is actually practised. The present (and past) education policies are inconsistent with a *genuine* regard for children's interests, particularly their interests in autonomy. There is evidence that the present moves towards what, in the United States is known as Community Mental Health, is also ideological.

One test for such an hypothesis would be to see whether the facilities which are now offered better serve the interests (in particular the autonomy interests) of their supposed beneficiaries than those offered by past services, or by an alternative policy. A further test would be to investigate whether other interests are served by the changes, than those of their supposed beneficiaries. Sedgwick (1982) is in no doubt that the drive to dismantle mental hospitals is ideological:

> 'In Britain no less than in the United States, "community care" and "the replacement of the mental hospital" were slogans which masked the growing depletion of real services for mental patients: the accumulating numbers of impaired, retarded and demented males in the prisons and common lodging-houses; the scarcity not only of local authority residential provision for the mentally disabled but of day centres and skilled social-work resources; the jettisoning of mental patients in their thousands into the isolated, helpless environment of their families of origin, who appealed in vain for hospital admission (even for a temporary period of respite), for counselling or support, and even for basic information and advice about the patient's diagnosis and medication.' (pp.193–4)

The final chapter of Sedgwick's book offers detailed and convincing evidence for the claims made in this quotation. Here are some considerations which support them.

It is clear that many of the old mental hospitals are now in need of drastic, and expensive repair. In any case they are expensive to maintain. As the age structure within society changes, so that a larger proportion of the population is elderly, the costs of psycho-geriatric care rapidly increase. Pushing the burden of mental health care back onto families and friends, and away from the hospitals is a way of saving on government expenditure. The majority of carers for the mentally ill at home are women – and with high unemployment, there are various moves to try to keep women at home and off the labour market. As the mentally ill are especially needy, and officially there is widespread concern for their welfare, it would not be politically wise to say simply that mental hospitals should close as a way of saving money.

There is evidence that one of the causes of the reduction in the hospital population is the extensive development and use of effective psychotropic drugs, which means that more people can exist outside mental institutions, in the absence of constant supervision, without endangering their own health or safety, or being an intolerable nuisance to those (probably women relatives) who provide their 'primary care'.

One danger of the widespread use of psychotropic drugs is the spectre of *Brave New World*: rather than trying to make society fit people, make people fit society. In the Brave New World of Huxley's novel most of the citizens took a drug, *soma*, whenever sadness, anxiety or agitation threatened. This mood-affecting drug immediately brought about feelings of well-being, and effectively eliminated the possibility of the citizens seeking to understand the world in which they lived, with its limitations. It kept them quiet.

Although the citizens of Brave New World were contented, their autonomy interests were seriously compromised, since they were denied the possibility of even developing the capacity for autonomy. It could be argued that the extensive dependence on psychotropic drugs for the treatment of the mentally disordered subverts *their* autonomy; or at any rate that it is inconsistent with a serious regard for their autonomy.

There has been a large increase since 1945 in reported 'mild' symptoms of mental disorder – particularly including anxiety, inability to relax, and feeling depressed. Many of these are frequently precipitated by social causes (see Brown and Harris, 1978). If they were tackled in a way which took seriously the importance of respecting individual's autonomy, they would properly be dealt with immediately by self-help programmes and perhaps psychotherapy, and in the long run by trying to bring about the social changes to remove the precipitating causes of the distress. Instead, the most common treatment is prescription of the tranquilliser diazepam, the most popular brand of which is Valium. Valium is in some respects like *soma* in that it provides effective relief of painful symptoms, and does very little for helping its supposed beneficiary to confront the causes of the problems which lead to the anxiety or other distress. As an emergency measure, to enable a patient to cope with a crisis before coming to grips with difficulties of life, Valium is unquestionably beneficial. But its widespread use – over a long period of time – as an alternative to psychotherapy, certainly subverts its user's autonomy interests. The suggestion that a person's problems will be dissolved away by his taking a pill often fails to describe reality, and is a way of fobbing off a patient, which is attractive to overstretched general practitioners with too many patients. The present lack of resources, which means that a health service doctor is able to spend only about five minutes per patient at surgeries, is incompatible with taking seriously the possibility of promoting the autonomy interests of patients suffering from anxiety or agitation.

Stronger drugs are used to control more serious disturbances. Chlorpromazine, encountered by many under the brand name 'Largactil' is widely used to tranquillise schizophrenics and other psychotics. One of its effects is to flatten the emotions. Again, in an emergency it is useful to have such a drug, to prevent a disturbed patient from harming himself or other people, without the need for physical restraints or padded cells. However, in the long run reliance on it may reduce the chances of the person taking it regaining autonomy. Largactil is used on long-term prison inmates and chronic mental patients, not to provide a cure, but effectively as an alternative to the cosh and the straitjacket. This is hardly consistent with concern for *their* autonomy interests.

There are several long-acting drugs which reduce the symptoms of schizophrenia, and do enable individuals to live outside institutions, who would, prior to the availability of the drug, probably have spent their lives inside. This does, in one sense increase their autonomy. No doubt these drugs are beneficial for many; but they are not always an unqualified success, as this (admittedly extreme) example quoted by Sedgwick suggests. These words were written in the British Medical Journal by a patient who had been on one of these drugs for some time: 'I think that the richness of my pre-injection days, even with brief outbursts of madness, is preferable to the numbed cabbage I have become.'

In addition to these there is a wide range of sleeping pills, or hypnotics. The main threat to autonomy posed by them is due to their unwelcome side-effects. Barbiturates can be physically addictive, so that takers become unable to give them up even if they want to; and there is evidence that they can cause cardio-vascular damage. These drugs are now less frequently prescribed, as alternative hypnotics, such as nitrazepam, with fewer attendant risks, are available. However, they are less effective for some insomniacs, and it is a moot point whether those who feel they need the more dangerous barbiturates in order to sleep should be allowed to exercise their autonomy in taking on the extra risk.

The final category of widely-used drugs for combatting mental maladies is the anti-depressants. There are several different types of anti-depressant, with differing advantages and drawbacks. Although some anti-depressants, such as the popular amitriptyline have a tranquillising effect, this is not true of all, and protriptyline is used to combat not only depression, but also related apathy and withdrawal. Lithium carbonate has been used to combat depression and mania. It has the drawback of being effective only within a narrow range of concentration within the blood. This requires frequent monitoring of those who take it.

I think the main problem is not the fact that such an array of powerful psychotropic drugs is available. By any standards the drugs can be very helpful – both in reducing mental pain, and in helping the mentally disturbed to regain their autonomy. The worry is that the drugs be used too often as an alternative to confronting the root causes of psychological distress, and thus treating mental patients as objects. There is a very real danger that people who cannot cope with society as it is, be drugged into a state of quiet acceptance, where they will not cause trouble, but hardly will live as autonomous individuals. But the case should not be overstated.

Those who believe there is a simple correlation between the availability of this wide range of psychic controllers and the drive to empty mental hospitals are in two camps. First are those who enthusiastically welcome the recent developments. They believe that the drugs render the need for custodial care obsolete, since they provide a satisfactory alternative, and enable the mentally disturbed to live safely and productively back in the community. The other group, whilst agreeing that the drugs have made it possible for state authorities to reduce the population of mental hospitals (which in itself is no bad thing), regard the widespread use of psychotropic drugs as most sinister.

The truth seems to be that there is no such simple correlation. For the reduction in the size of the mental hospital population in Britain and the United States throughout the 1950's and 1960's was great, whereas during the same period there was an increase in France and other European countries which had access to the same drugs (see Sedgwick, 1982, p.198).

The most plausible explanation for the recent popularity among governments of the community mental health project, at least in the last decade, is the economic argument. As governments seek to reduce public expenditure they reduce the funds available for welfare, and in particular for mental health care. If patients can be taken out of institutions and cared for by their relatives, the financial burden on the omnipresent 'taxpayer' and 'ratepayer' is reduced. Scull (1977) defends this analysis in considerable detail.

There is, then, evidence that the move to put mental patients back into the community does save money at a time when governments are seeking to reduce their expenditure. On the other hand, it is clear that simply removing mental patients from hospital does not always serve their interests, either in pleasant mental states or in autonomy. Wing (1978) mentions the concern of the New York Times with practices 'in which patients released from state hospitals often wind up in cheap hotels or other poor accommodations, get little medical help and eventually return to hospitals' (p.214).

Of course there will always be some patients who benefit from moves to reduce the population of mental hospitals. For example there are stories of people incarcerated in British mental hospitals for 40 years or more, for alleged 'moral crimes', such as having a baby out of wedlock. Such people have suffered greatly through being in institutional care, and much publicity has been given to the laudable efforts to restore to them sufficient autonomy to enable them to live in the community. However, these successes should not disguise the fact that resources for many in need of help outside hospital are woefully inadequate, while investment within mental hospitals, at least in Britain, has been drastically reduced – partly through the rhetoric of the new emphasis on community care.

Taking seriously the autonomy of mental patients

I have described some of the shortcomings of contemporary policy in regard to mental handicap and mental illness. In both cases it seems that the autonomy interests of sufferers from these conditions are not properly met. How might it be possible to give proper respect to the autonomy of those who suffer from mental illness?

There is, and no doubt will continue to be, considerable controversy over the causes of mental disorders. Consequently there will continue to be disagreement about what constitute the best ways of preventing the disorders in the first place, and of treating them once they have become manifest.

However, a striking fact about the distribution of types of psychiatric and psychotherapeutic care available is that there are widespread differences between the care for the wealthy minority who have private treatment, and the majority who rely on state resources. Although it is possible that some wealthy people are merely duped into spending lots of their money on worthless, though fashionable remedies, there must be *some* presumption that the facilities chosen by the better off are better than those, also available to, but rejected by, them, which are widely used in the public sector.

In the United States there is a marked difference between the treatment which poorer members of society are likely to receive in state institutions, and the psychotherapy which tends to be available to those in social classes 1 and 2. According to H. Davidson (1967):

> '90% of training time is spent in teaching its happy beneficiaries to handle only 5% of the patients. The remaining 10% of the trainees have to treat the remaining 95% of the patients.'
> (Quoted in Wing, 1978, p.210)

In another study carried out in New Haven Connecticut in 1950 and 1975, although it was shown that there were widespread changes in policy – particularly in regard to the community health programme, the class inequalities of mental health care persisted. (See Hollingshead and Redlich, 1958; and Redlich and Kellert, 1978.) In particular, the earlier research showed that electro-convulsive therapy, drug treatment and brain surgery were more widely used on members of social class 5, whereas psychotherapy was on the whole available only for those in the higher classes.

Evidence concerning the efficacy of the various kinds of psychotherapy remains highly controversial. However, psycho-therapy does have as a prime aim the development of the autonomy of the person in therapy. Psychoanalysis, for example, aims to give the person in analysis an understanding of the root causes of his distress. Whereas it is true that mere understanding is insufficient for autonomy, it is a necessary condition. Drug therapy in the absence of what is sometimes called 'the talking treatment' may not even aim at producing insight. Admittedly, interminable psychoanalysis *can* itself generate heteronomy in the patient who, as it were, becomes addicted to his analysis. However, this is not intrinsic to the process of seeking out and confronting directly the causes of one's own irrationality-produced distress. Whereas psychotherapy does not always achieve its aim of restoring an agent's autonomy, this goal may not even be on the agenda of more common treatments.

In the domain of physical illness, the principle of equal respect for people requires that ability to pay should not be a determinant of whether a person receives the best available treatment for a condition such as kidney failure. Dialysis machines and kidneys for transplant are distributed, supposedly, on medical grounds, not according (directly) to the wealth of those who need them. In the nineteenth century, when the huge asylums were built, housing thousands of the poor mentally disturbed, there were places for rich mentally ill people to go, to be treated with dignity, in a way which would enable them to regain their self-respect. Here is a description of one – the most expensive private asylum in England:

'At the asylum itself, every effort was made to occupy and amuse the patients. Lectures were given on popular subjects. There were fortnightly concerts in the summer, "as many as thirty-six patients took part in them". Many patients dined regularly with their physicians. "An excellent theatre with scenery" was constructed for the use of the patients. Some patients were "taken to festivities in the neighbourhood, cricket matches, archery, fetes, flower shows, and others have been taken out for picnics". Horses, donkeys, and carriages were available for riding, and a pack of hounds for hunting. . . . In short, while moral treatment may have disappeared without trace in the public asylums, it was applied with a vengeance at some of the private ones. In the words of the Commissioners, "the recreation grounds are large and well-adapted to restore

health to diseased minds . . . and we can speak in high terms
. . . of the efforts made to promote the recovery and welfare of
those placed here for treatment".' (Scull, 1979, p.207)

It would be quite unreasonable to expect this level of luxury to be
extended to all mental patients in a society which had not
abolished poverty. However, to treat people suffering from
mental disorders with dignity requires the allocation of a lot of
time – and this is what is noticeably lacking for most mental
patients in the public sector. Here is an extract from a submission
by the Royal College of Psychiàtrists in 1974:

'The average standard of psychiatric practice in Britain is
abysmally low. Psychiatrists themselves are sometimes reluctant
to make this admission, but the evidence is overwhelming. In
an average mental hospital, a long-stay patient is likely to see a
doctor for only ten minutes or so every three months. Even a
recently admitted patient is seen by a doctor on average of only
20 minutes each week. This tenuous contact between the
psychiatrist and his patient is reflected in the case-notes which
are often almost uninformative. Scandals about the ill-treatment
of patients in mental hospitals, including those of relatively
good reputation, occur with monotonous regularity. Even when
the medical staff are not directly involved in these incidents,
their occurrence reflects the unavailability of doctors to guide
nursing and other staff.' (Quoted in Clare, 1976, p.370)

Care both within and outside mental hospitals is for most people
inadequate – because inadequately resourced. Psychiatrists spend
such a relatively short time with their patients because they have
too many patients to cope with. It is also true that the case loads
of social workers are too high to enable them to give proper
weight to the autonomy interests of their clients. In such an
environment a tendency to rely too heavily on 'brief therapies'
which will at least relieve the pressure of too many patients and
clients is inevitable, even in those cases where this is incompatible
with a serious regard for the autonomy interests of patients or
clients.

A small step towards respecting autonomy would be for
doctors, as a general rule, to explain to patients what the different

treatment options might be – with strengths and weaknesses, so that the patient might take a more active role in determining her fate. Of course this may not always be possible, but very often drugs are prescribed without even trying to explain to the patient what the expected effects of the drug are likely to be.

I have spent most of this chapter talking about treatment of mental disorders once they have arisen. Clearly, in the field of mental as well as physical health the prevention of illness is preferable to cure. There are close connections between various mental disturbances and environmental factors which could be changed (see Brown and Harris, 1978, for an account of the social origins of depression in women). One of their findings was that much depression in women is (unsurprisingly one might think) brought about by their suffering from the loss of valued objects, partly as a result of poverty and social isolation. They write:

'the issue of treatment must be considered side by side with the issue of prevention. The implication of these results for the latter can only be the need for wider social and political changes which would mean that fewer people experienced provoking agents and fewer people were vulnerable in the first place. These findings provide backing for many reforms in our current social organisation, increases in the number of nursery school places and the number of part-time employment opportunities for women being some obvious candidates. They point, too, to the large areas of loneliness and isolation which exist amid our so-called affluence, and to the important role they play in determining family health. To combat these, and to build a sense of mastery and self-esteem, which will render every member of the community more resilient to the buffets of experience, requires more than comforting talk in a surgery, although even this is all too often not available. (pp.292–3)

There is evidence that schizophrenia is precipitated, amongst vulnerable people, by impossible and contradictory demands being put upon them within the family. Both depression and schizophrenia are serious destroyers of people's autonomy.

In so far as mental illness destroys autonomy, and is caused by social determinants, the best way of taking seriously the autonomy interests of the potentially mentally ill would be to change the environmental factors which cause it. In a sense, arguments about whether the main treatment of psychological disorder should take place in special mental hospitals, psychiatric units of general hospitals, out-patient clinics, day-centres, or at home, pale into insignificance before the environmental problems. The most effective way to reduce the suffering caused by cholera was to make clean water available to everyone, rather than just to find a better way of treating the disease once it had set in. To tackle the causes of many mental disorders would be a far more major project, which would require a radical restructuring of society, including a massive redistribution of social goods; and the obstacles to achieving this within the ground rules of liberal democratic society as we know it, are so great as to be practically insuperable.

Conclusion

The autonomy of the mentally handicapped is impaired because they lack the intellectual capacity to reason effectively, particularly in regard to complex new situations. This does not mean that they are totally incompetent, or that they have no autonomy interests. General restrictions on the liberty of the mildly retarded, which supposedly protect them against exploitation in fact are, in many cases an affront to their autonomy. Perhaps, given the rest of the way society is organised, their mental state interests are served by such a general restriction, but their autonomy interests certainly aren't. The general argument for restricting the liberty of the mildly retarded on the grounds that the restriction is necessary to prevent exploitation must not obscure the fact that current social and economic arrangements are organised in a way which suits the convenience of the 'normal' at the expense of the vital interests in autonomy of the 'handicapped'. In a society which is governed by the laws of the 'free market' this inequality will continue.

I rejected the view which claims there is a distinction, of great moral significance, between ascriptions of 'objective' physical illness, and ascriptions of 'value-relative' mental illness. I argued that both sorts of ascriptions are value-relative, whilst rejecting the view that this means ascriptions are automatically arbitrary or unwarranted. Describing someone, perhaps oneself, as mentally ill is not automatically an insult to their autonomy. Whether or not it is depends on one's view of illness.

One of the distinctive properties of much mental illness is the loss of autonomy for the mentally ill person (irrespective of whether he has been labelled 'mentally ill'). Much interest in the issue of mental illness and autonomy has focused on the vexed question of compulsory treatment. I have argued that compulsory treatment does not in itself violate the principle of respect for autonomy. It may be necessary either to protect the interests (in autonomy or welfare) of the patient, or to protect the interests of others. Although questions about the justification for compulsory treatment are very important, my focus in this chapter has been elsewhere – on the treatment which is available to those deemed 'mentally ill'.

The main conclusion to be drawn in regard to the interests of this book is that the services provided for the majority of mentally ill people in Britain and the United States are certainly inadequate, if a gauge of their adequacy is measured by reference to restoration of autonomy. There has been, and continues to be, a great discrepancy between the facilities available to the wealthy minority and those available for the majority. Although the rhetoric of liberating people from incarceration in huge asylums, to enable them to live once more in the community, is impressive, the reality of recent changes is that the problems of the mentally ill have not been confronted adequately.

Once again, it appears that the societies of the free world, where individual autonomy is regarded as of paramount value, are unable to take seriously the autonomy interests of a substantial minority of their population. Market forces do not protect the vital interests of the poor mentally disordered.

10 False Consciousness and Emancipation

'is it not the supreme and most insidious exercise of power to prevent people, to whatever degree, from having grievances by shaping their perceptions, cognitions and preferences in such a way that they accept their role in the existing order of things, either because they can see or imagine no alternative to it, or because they see it as natural and unchangeable, or because they value it as divinely ordained and beneficial?' (Steven Lukes, 1974)

I mentioned in the Introduction C. B. Macpherson's (1977) view that there is a deep tension between liberal democracy's belief in the equal rights of all to self-determination and its association with capitalism. I have, in the previous two chapters, argued that at least two minority groups – children and the mentally disordered – do not have their autonomy interests properly protected in liberal democratic societies. Although it would be quite beyond the scope of this book to try to prove that they *could not* properly be protected in an inegalitarian capitalist society, the thesis that they could not is at least plausible. In this chapter I wish to discuss an alleged problem, which appears to be far more serious for liberal democracy than the (mis)treatment of children and the mentally disordered. It is arguable that there is a much broader section of the population who have little control over their own lives: no justification for their lack of autonomy is offered – indeed, their lack of autonomy is scarcely recognised. These are the masses, who, according to some radical socialists, suffer from 'false consciousness'. If indeed it is true that liberal democratic societies fail to defend and promote what I have called 'the general autonomy', then those who share the liberal commitment to autonomy should seriously consider radical change to the structure of such societies. Were there a genuine conflict between capitalism and the general autonomy, then those who seriously believe in the liberal principles of autonomy should reject capitalism rather than abandon autonomy. The problem for those who reject capitalism is that socialism, the most plausible alternative to capitalism, never seems to reach the top of the agenda of any major political party within liberal democracies, and the transition to socialism seems as far away as ever.

My aim in this chapter is to discuss the problem of 'false consciousness' in so far as it is relevant to the ethics of radical social change. My arguments are aimed at those who share the liberal belief in the vital importance of autonomy. Although such a belief has strong implications for the kind of society one would want (it would, for instance, be incompatible with acceptance of a fascist state), this chapter is mainly concerned with the ethics of social transformation, in a world where people's autonomy appears to be undermined by the choices which they themselves make in elections and over other life-affecting matters.

False consciousness

I shall start with a discussion of 'false consciousness'. 'False consciousness' is a term which was originally used in a letter from Friedrich Engels to Franz Mehring on 14 July 1893. He wrote:

> 'Ideology is a process accomplished by the so-called thinker consciously, it is true, but with false consciousness. The real motive forces impelling him remain unknown to him: otherwise it simply would not be an ideological process. Hence he imagines false or seeming motive forces.' (Quoted in Lewy, 1982, p.3)

The citizen suffering from false consciousness is mistaken about 'the real motive forces impelling him'. What does this mean? The classic example is a slave who does not question her slavery. She believes that it is 'natural' for some people to be subservient to others. She thinks that she is working for a pittance, because this is the way people of her kind have always, should always, and will always continue to live. An industrial worker may believe that impartial 'market forces' have always, will always, and should always determine the conditions in which goods are produced and distributed. The slave and the worker each have a false belief about history, a dubious normative belief, and a disputable belief about the future. These, so the false consciousness thesis goes, prevent them from understanding why they are in the position they are in, and how they might get out of it. It is an obstacle to their pursuit of their own real interests, and is incompatible with their autonomy.

The ancestry of the concept goes back at least as far as Plato and his myth of the cave. Since Engels's time the term 'false consciousness' has taken on a wider connotation, meaning something like 'mistaken beliefs about what is in one's real interests'. One of the pervasive features of false consciousness is that it restricts people's vision of feasible alternatives. Thus, it is possible that preferences revealed by choices, such as votes in elections, may not be a statement of the voters' true interests. Acceptance of this possibility calls into question the legitimacy of the claims made by the governments of liberal democratic societies, to represent the interests of the majority of the community (even when they *are* elected by a majority of the community).

As early as 1845 Marx put forward the view that something like false consciousness will be widespread in any class-divided society:

'The ideas of the ruling class are, in every age, the ruling ideas: i.e. the class which is the dominant *material* force in society is at the same time its dominant *intellectual* force. The class which has the means of material production at its disposal, has control at the same time over the means of mental production, so that in consequence the ideas of those who lack the means of mental production are, in general, subject to it. The dominant ideas are nothing more than the ideal expression of the dominant material relationships grasped as ideas, and thus of the relationships which make one class the ruling one; they are consequently the ideas of its dominance.' (Marx, 1845–6, p.78)

This does not mean that it is impossible for other views to develop. However, it could explain why revolutionary policies are rarely popular. As long as those seeking a radical transformation of society do not rule the society, their ideas will always be minority views. Radicals can argue that the autonomy of the majority of citizens in liberal democratic societies is severely undermined by their false consciousness. They accept the *status quo*, through possessing an inadequate understanding of the true nature of their own desire formation and about the possibilities of political change.

On the other hand, defenders of liberal democracy argue that the false consciousness thesis is a thinly disguised tool of oppression, used by authoritarian anti-democrats, who are condemned to be in a minority by the genuine repugnance of their views. The claim that vast numbers of people can suffer from false consciousness is just an excuse for imposing unpopular measures on an unwilling population. They may point to the history of the Soviet Union, and the actions of the Bolshevik party under Lenin and Stalin. In 1917 the Bolshevik Party represented a tiny minority of opinion within what was to become the Soviet Union. Lenin believed that by its own efforts the working class would never come to a true understanding of its oppression. There was a need for a vanguard party of professional revolutionaries, who could seize power, and then bring education for true political consciousness to the masses. The bloody history of Stalinism is a fitting testimony to the claims of the vanguard party to serve the true interests of the masses. Millions of peasants who resisted the forced collectivisation and industrialisation died as a result of the policy of 'forcing people to be free', and millions more were imprisoned or exiled. People are the best judges of their own interests, and in so far as respect is to be shown for the autonomy of citizens, their expressed preferences should be taken as definitive of their interests.

The paradox of emancipation

Winston Churchill is reported to have said that democracy is the worst form of government – apart from all the rest. Whether or not Western liberal democracies really are democratic is a topic for another book. However, the history of the Soviet Union and its satellites in Eastern Europe has certainly provided evidence that the attempt to impose 'communism' from above does not lead to an unqualified benefit for those 'emancipated'. The Stalinist version of 'communism' is, for most citizens of liberal democracies, including many radical socialists, less attractive than liberal democracy, with all the flaws of the latter. On the other hand, there is a widespread belief among anti-Stalinist socialists that false consciousness is rampant within the populations of liberal democratic societies. The recognition that it is morally and politically unacceptable to try to impose political changes on an unwilling population, combined with a belief that false consciousness is common leads to what Benton (1982) has called 'the paradox of emancipation'. Suppose your goal is the emancipation of the majority of the population from the false consciousness from which they suffer, what should be your strategy? If you play according to the rules of liberal democracy, the odds are so heavily stacked against you that you will almost certainly lose. For the 'means of mental production' rest in the hands of those who would prevent radical social change. On the other hand, if you abandon those rules, it is hard to avoid the authoritarian excesses of Stalinism. Benton puts it like this, perhaps a little too strongly:

> 'Since the political values of the radical critics are, generally speaking, egalitarian, democratic, and/or libertarian, they are caught in a paradox: if they are to remain true to their political values they may implement no changes without the consent of those who are affected by them, and if they seek to implement no such changes, then they acquiesce in the persistence of a social system radically at odds with their political values.' (p.15)

Is 'emancipation', therefore, an illusion, which should be dropped from the political agenda? I believe that the principle of respect for autonomy offers a way of allaying liberal and libertarian fears, whilst rejecting the view that people's present preferences should always have to determine what is legitimately on the political agenda.

Real interests

Radical socialists are unhappy to accept people's expressed preferences as settling the question of what policies should be pursued in a society, because they believe that people may be mistaken about their real interests, and thus that the pursuit of their preferences may not be best for them on particular occasions. Liberals, on the other hand, following in the tradition of Mill, believe that people's expressed preferences should be overridden only to prevent harm to others. They are prepared to make an exception to this principle in the case of children and the mentally disordered. According to the disclaimer to the Liberty Principle, those who are

> 'in a state to require being taken care of by others, must be protected against their own actions as well as against external injury.' (Mill, 1859, p.73)

The Liberty Principle derives its moral appeal from two sources. First there is the belief that, because autonomy is a vital interest, it is better for people to make their own choices, even if this is more painful for them. The other is the belief that even if paternalistic intervention is acceptable in principle, as a policy, it is likely to do more harm than good, on account of various human fallibilities. These grounds for accepting the Liberty Principle are, of course, consistent with the view that people may be mistaken about their own true interests.

Any political philosophy which seeks morally to justify a policy of radical social change must, I think, rely on the claim that people can be mistaken about their own real interests. This certainly would be true if the dominant ideas in any society are the ideas of those who control the means of material production. A little thought shows that people can be mistaken about their real interests.

Mill, as we have seen, discusses the case of someone who wants to step onto an unsafe bridge, being unaware of its condition. He thinks it is in his interests to step onto the bridge, but it manifestly isn't. Why not? Because if he steps onto it he will get wet, suffer discomfort, and possibly drown. He wants to step onto the bridge only because of a simple, though understandable belief that the bridge is safe. The mistaken belief about his interests is uncontroversial, and, given that he is neither a lunatic nor intending to commit suicide, nor someone with a special project in mind, he will agree that stepping onto the bridge would be against his interests. Suppose there is no time or opportunity to warn him: it is legitimate to use force to prevent him – not least out of respect for his autonomy.

There are many sorts of factual error which people can and do make about what is in their interests. Here are a few. Alice's pint of milk, which she thinks is safe to drink, unknown to her, is contaminated with brucillosis. Bill buys a stereo system from store *A* for £200, when he could have bought an identical system from store *B* for £150. He was unaware of this alternative. Carol is unaware that smoking has been proved to be hazardous to health. She doesn't realise that continuing to smoke may be against her interests. David supports Party *X* rather than Party *Y* in a particular election campaign, because he believes that Party *X* will reduce unemployment and keep inflation down, and that Party *Y* will do neither. Low unemployment and low inflation would be more in his interests than high unemployment and inflation. He could be mistaken about the relative abilities and intentions of the two parties.

In the first two cases the relevant information would almost certainly be gratefully accepted, and, unless it was too late, Alice would not drink the milk, and Bill would not buy the system from store *B*. The smoking case is more complicated; for the evidence is still somewhat controversial, and many smokers are so hooked on the habit that they are either unable or unwilling to think rationally about the practice. Nevertheless, suppose that Carol's continuing to smoke does give her lung cancer in 15 years' time. She then concedes that smoking was against her best interests, and she was earlier mistaken. There is no special theoretical difficulty in accepting that her later view is correct. David's case is also complicated – because there are many reasons for allegiances to political parties, and outcomes are very difficult to predict.

The recognition that people can be mistaken about their best interests, although showing that paternalistic restriction of people's liberty is not obviously wrong in principle, does not commit one to the view that such restrictions are always justifiable when, in their absence, people are likely to act against their best interests. There are two main reasons for this.

First, as Mill claims (1859, p.140), there is a great danger that once the principle of such interferences is accepted, people are very likely to intervene in the wrong place, or in the wrong manner. A more successful policy would be to leave people well alone, except in extreme circumstances. The other reason is that although it might be more in a person's interests to *choose* policy *X* rather than policy *Y*, it could well be against his interests to be *forced* to adopt *X* rather than *Y*. To be forced into doing something against one's will is, *prima facie*, a personal insult and affront to one's autonomy and dignity. So, even though continuing to smoke may be less in Carol's interests than giving up, it might be more in her interests than being forced to stop.

The above cases, where a failure to recognise what is in one's best interests is due to a readily identifiable factual error, are relatively uncontroversial. In one sense they could all be described as 'false consciousness'. However, in the context of the debate between radical and liberal there is, at least according to the radical, a further kind of mistake which people make about what is in their real interests. Typically, this is a mistake about the relative desirability of different ways of life, usually shaped by beliefs about what is 'feasible'. Such beliefs in turn very often rest on further beliefs about what is 'natural'. Historical examples include a belief in the divine right of kings to absolute power on earth; a belief that a woman's proper place is in the home; and a belief that it is unnatural for 'working people' to manage their own affairs at work.

The radical claim is that people may be and very often are, mistaken, not just about the best means for *achieving* their goals, but mistaken in the very *selection* of their goals. The majority of a servant class may have no desire to become emancipated from their position of subservience. They might think that such a possibility is quite outside the realms of the natural or the feasible. Yet perhaps their interests would be better served by having more adventurous ambitions. Where might the widespread acceptance by a servant class, of their subservience, come from?

Well, according to Marx, as we have seen, 'The dominant ideas are nothing more than the ideal expression of the dominant material relationships, the dominant material relationships grasped as ideas, and thus of the relationships which make one class the ruling class'. To put it crudely, it is clearly in the interests of the aristocracy and the bourgeoisie to have willing servants and 'wage slaves', who believe that it is 'natural', or 'right and proper', or at least inevitable, that they serve their masters. In truth, it is neither natural *nor* unnatural for some people to be the servants of others. Whether or not there will be servants is a function of the way a society is organised. The willing servants, who would not want 'liberation' from servitude, even if it were offered, do not realise their true interests, because they have mistaken beliefs about what might constitute a good life for them – or at least a better life.

Perhaps the *locus classicus* for the false consciousness thesis is Herbert Marcuse's book (1964), *One Dimensional Man*. In it he argues that modern industrial societies have produced in their populations false needs, the pursuit of which are damaging to the real interests of the individuals who pursue them, and to other members of the society. I think a need is a necessary condition for the attainment of a desirable goal, or at least a goal which is thought to be desirable. According to Marcuse:

'We may distinguish both true and false needs. "False" are those which are superimposed upon the individual by particular social interests in his repression: the needs which perpetuate toil, aggressiveness, misery and injustice. Their satisfaction might be most gratifying to the individual, but this happiness is not a condition which has to be maintained and protected if it serves to arrest the development of the ability (his own and others) to recognise the disease of the whole and grasp the chances of curing the disease. The result then is euphoria in unhappiness. Most of the prevailing needs to relax, to have fun, to behave and consume in accordance with the advertisements, to love and hate what others love and hate, belong to this category of false needs.

Such needs have a societal content and function which are determined by external powers over which the individual has no control; the development and satisfaction of these needs is heteronomous.' (Marcuse, 1964, pp.4–5)

The rhetoric is different, but the implicit claims about the necessity of autonomy for happiness are strongly reminiscent of Mill.

Marcuse would argue that the main reason for the relative stability of liberal democratic predominantly capitalist societies is that they have been fairly efficient at satisfying the want-given needs of their populations, or at least it is widely believed that they are more so than any rival systems. For example, the vast majority of people in these societies live in households with refridgerators, washing machines and telephones. There is a fear, how well-grounded, I am not sure, that a socialist society would, at least at first, be incompatible with these high material standards of living. Marcuse might claim that the need in Western Europe and North America to achieve self-esteem by surrounding oneself with status-symbol consumer durables is a 'false need'. It is created by 'external powers', and it is against people's real interests to attach such great importance to, say, having one's own motor car, swimming pool, or whatever. Moreover, as long as people are preoccupied with the pursuit of such needs, they will not spend their time and energy on intrinsically more rewarding activities. Our society is to be condemned because it creates widespread false needs which lead people not to pursue their own best (real) interests, but to become passive consumers.

The main objection to the false consciousness thesis is that it has proved difficult, if not impossible for radicals to produce a theory of true versus false needs, and of real versus apparent interests, which is resistant to charges of arbitrariness, special pleading or sour grapes. To take the above quotation from Marcuse: what evidence is there that needs which perpetuate aggressiveness are somehow not genuine? The world would, perhaps, be a happier place if people were less aggressive. However, although human shortcomings may not be 'natural' and therefore immutable by social change, this does not make them false or inauthentic. The real interests of saints may be expected to differ from those of ordinary fallible mere mortals. The accounts of 'true needs' and 'real interests' divorce what is supposed to be in people's interests too much from the actual people under consideration. The first danger a radical socialist is likely to face is that she just cites a set of possible human goals, personally appealing to her, which she then elevates to the status of being in other people's 'real' interests. The more serious danger is that this may lead to a misplaced 'justification' of the coercion or manipulation of people.

Steven Lukes (1974) is well aware of this difficulty, and has tried to produce a definition of real interests which allows for the kind of mistake about real interests mentioned above, whilst not divorcing people's supposed real interests too much from their actual selves. Lukes identifies the radical about power and interests as someone who maintains:

> 'that men's wants may themselves be a product of a system which works against their interests, and, in such cases, relates the latter to what they would want and prefer were they able to make the choice.' (p.34)

In a footnote on the same page he quotes with approval William Connolly's 'first approximation' to a definition of real interests:

> 'Policy x is more in A's interest than policy y, if A, were he to experience the *results* of x and y, would *choose x* as the result he would rather have for himself.' (Connolly, 1972, p.472) [See also Connolly, 1983]

This account is reassuring in its insistence that special facts about A fix what is in his interests. This excludes the possibility of it turning out that, for example, living on a collective farm is more in someone's interests than running their own smallholding, even though this person would, having experienced both, still prefer the latter. This, of course, is quite consistent with a reverse pattern of interests for others.

It is also good that Connolly expresses interests comparatively. This avoids problems associated with trying to give a precise account of what would constitute *the* definitive set of real interests of a person, group or class, whilst it still allows one to make critical judgments about particular policies.

There are, however, serious difficulties with this account. Is a knock on the head more in someone's interests than not receiving the blow? Suppose that after the blow the person becomes a contented semi-vegetable, so that he is content to stay where he is. He even prefers his present existence to the alternative of a 'normal' life outside. Suppose that you knew this would be the effect of giving someone a blow on the head. This raises, amongst other things, the problem of picking out just *which* results of a policy a person must be presumed to experience, in order for one to arrive at a judgment of his real interests. The results of any policy have ramifications which spread even beyond the life of any given individual. Are a person's real interests to be determined by speculating on his attitude to the policies, having experienced the whole range of their results? A being with such a range of experiences would be someone quite different from the person whose interests are in question, someone with infinite capacities. On the other hand, if we are to select just some of the results of the policies, which are to be regarded as salient? There seems to be no non-arbitrary restriction on which results are to count. Experiences can drastically affect what is in a person's interests by changing his desires or values.

Benton (1982) has a barrage of criticisms of the Connolly–Lukes position, one of which is the following:

'Not only is it necessarily an external observer or analyst who makes the judgement as to what the actor would do under certain counterfactual conditions, but it is also the external observer who decides (through the choice of conception of interests) which among the infinitely large class of counterfactual conditions are to be the privileged ones.' (Benton, 1982, pp. 25–6)

The thrust of this objection is that the account of real interests offered does not, in the end, allow for sufficient weight to be given to the individual's autonomy. It appears to open the door to just the sort of coercion of people 'in their own best interests' which it was introduced to avoid.

So, after all, the analysis seems to give too much to the would-be tyrant, because it allows that a policy may be in someone's interests, even though it is never ever wanted by him. On the other hand, it seems to concede too much to the anti-radical, since it does not exclude the possibility of real interests being set by just the kind of suspect desire which the account was supposed to avoid. The Connolly–Lukes strategy is open to the same objection as that which befell the Deliberative Theory and Mill's attempt to show conclusively that autonomy is a vital interest of human beings. They all place too great a weight on reference to hypothetical desires. But if such appeals are unsuccessful, is there any room for a justifiable radical social critique.

Perhaps the radical can concede more to the liberal than seemed possible at the outset, without abandoning the possibility of justifying a commitment to radical social change in the face of widespread quiescence towards the *status quo*.

The key lies in the liberal's commitment to the value of autonomy, which I think is at the heart of the liberal opposition to state paternalism. The implications of taking seriously the importance of autonomy are radical.

Autonomy, interests and perfectionism

According to a popular view, liberalism is a political philosophy which is neutral about competing conceptions of what constitutes a good life. What may be good for one person may be hopeless for another. Thus liberalism is supposed to avoid the problems of false consciousness and real interests which beset radicals, particularly radical democratic socialists. In the tradition of Mill, contemporary writers such as Rawls (1971) and Dworkin (1978) have sought to derive substantive principles of justice and liberty from appeal to principles of rationality, which purport to be independent of any particular conception of a good or worthwhile life. Liberalism is thus supposed to have a universal appeal. However, this view is, I think, hard to defend.

In his book *Liberty, Equality and Perfectionism* (1979), Vinit Haksar convincingly argues that liberal principles of liberty and equality can be defended only by appeal (perhaps tacit and disguised appeal) to 'perfectionist' principles. A perfectionist principle is one which is designed to promote human excellence in some field, independently of whether it is actually desired; perhaps by bringing it about that it is desired. Haksar claims that autonomy has to be valued in its own right, in order to get the liberal programme off the ground. However, the belief that an autonomous life is more worthwhile than other forms of existence cannot be established by rational argument, or by direct appeal to human nature, alone. This view is supported by our criticism of attempts to provide theories of rationality and real interests which appeal to people's hypothetical desires and preferences (see the discussion of hypothetical preferences in Chapters 3 and 4).

The most substantial liberal objection to radical theories which place great weight on appeal to people's supposed real interests and true needs, is that they threaten to legitimise policies which do not respect people's autonomy.

Although the liberal belief in autonomy may not be justifiable by appeal to general principles of rationality or humanity, the claim that people have an interest in autonomy, whether they realise it or not, is unique in that if people's supposed interests in it are satisfied, there is no question of their autonomy being not treated with sufficient seriousness. My autonomy cannot be violated by my autonomy interests being satisfied, although of course, on occasion, I may be prevented from doing what I (perhaps autonomously) want to do.

Recall that Marcuse describes two salient features of so-called 'false needs' – they 'perpetuate toil, aggressiveness, misery and injustice'; and they are 'determined by external powers over which the individual has no control; the development and satisfaction of these needs is heteronomous'.

The liberal objection to the first part of the characterisation is that the fact that there are needs, the pursuit of which leads to undesirable states of affairs, does not in itself call into question the genuineness of the needs. A desire to own a conspicuously expensive car may drive people to aggressive competitiveness which is worse for all than more co-operative behaviour. If people could be more co-operative then they would all (as a totality) do better at satisfying their needs than if they continue to be competitive. This does not mean that these desires and their pursuit are not successful attempts to satisfy real needs.

What about the other part – the claim that 'the development and satisfaction of these needs is heteronomous'? Even if the needs created, say, by manipulative advertising campaigns are nonetheless genuine needs, it could still be argued that their *production* is an assault upon people's autonomy.

To take an extreme example: A drug pedlar persuades a youth to try smoking heroin, by pointing out its attractions, and telling him that the pleasures of 'chasing the dragon' are as great as those of injecting, without the attendant risks of infection and addiction. The youth smokes some heroin, finds the experience thrilling, tries it again . . . and again . . . and develops a craving for the drug. The pedlar then employs the youth as a junior salesman of heroin, a job which the youth gratefully accepts as an effective way of satisfying his need for heroin.

It is plausible to maintain that before he met the pedlar, the youth neither wanted nor needed to take heroin. After talking to the pedlar he wanted to try it. He then developed a genuine need for the drug. Having another smoke certainly would satisfy his interest in avoiding stomach cramps and other withdrawal symptoms; and the pedlar was able to satisfy these needs. Let us now assume that the youth is not entirely dissatisfied with his lifestyle, and resists suggestions that he might go on a 'cold turkey' treatment to give up heroin.

Envisage an argument between a 'radical' socialist and a 'liberal', who both agreed that autonomy is a vital interest. What might they say? The 'radical' could say that the youth's need for heroin was a false need, and that continuing with his habit was against his real interests. The 'liberal' would affirm that the addict really needed heroin, and that supplying it was now more in his interests than withholding it.

However, there is one crucial point about which 'liberal' and 'radical' could agree. The behaviour of the pedlar is to be deplored. The 'radical' maintains his conduct is deplorable because it leads the youth to develop false needs, the pursuit of which is against his real interests (even after he has acquired the 'false' needs). The 'liberal' deplores the conduct because it creates needs the having of which undermines the youth's autonomy. The 'liberal' may claim that, once he has become addicted, the youth's interests, including autonomy interests, are best served by not forcing him to abandon his habit. The pedlar has behaved deplorably, first, because he has manipulated the youth by a deliberate failure to explain the real risks. Second, and perhaps more important, he has brought about a situation where the youth's vital interests in autonomy conflict drastically with his vital mental state interests. For once a person has become a heroin addict, regaining autonomy is extremely painful. Prior to becoming addicted it is easier for a person to do the things he believes are intrinsically worthwhile. The addiction is against the person's interests because it creates a conflict between vital interests, which prevents his attaining happiness.

It is possible to condemn the heroin trade without relying on the view that it is against the real interests of those hooked on heroin to continue taking the drug; continuing to take the drug may or may not be against the addict's interests (given that he has become an addict). By analogy, one can reason that the process of desire and need formation in a society is to be condemned, without having to rely on the claim that it is against the real interests of individuals in that society to act in pursuit of these undesirable desires and deplorable needs.

A less extreme example: John was raised on an estate located next to a car factory. Most of the employed adults on the estate worked in the factory. Following local traditions, he left school at 16 to start work on the production line. His expectations were to be an unskilled labourer on the production line throughout his working life. Within five years he had become accustomed to having his own television, video recorder, stereo system, and running a car. By now he found the work on the line monotonous and soul-destroying, but he needed to carry on with it in order to pay for the consumer products which he regarded as so important. Indeed, he had started working overtime in order to pay for the car.

Does he suffer from false consciousness? Is it against his interests to continue working at the factory? Is there anything wrong, for John, with the process of socialisation, and the socio-economic system which led him to work on the production line in pursuit of consumer durables from the age of 16?

On the analysis offered here, it is most likely to be more in John's interests, (given his pattern of desires, and likely available options) to continue working at the factory than to give up his job. In so far as he is aware of this, he does not suffer from false consciousness, in the sense of mistaken belief about what is in his real interests. On the other hand, there is much to say in criticism of the socialisation and socio-economic system which helped to chart out his life for him. By the age of 21 he has a set of dependencies which tie him down (on pain of pain!) to work which he finds intrinsically unsatisfying. Perhaps his education at school did not encourage critical thinking, the ability to question taken-for-granted assumptions, the ability to reject conformity to expected norms. His love of consumer durables was in part created by sales promotion campaigns, exploiting the mechanism of non-rational association of ideas. He is by now far from autonomous. Most of his time is spent in an activity which he finds soul-destroying, which is necessary to satisfy desires which have been created by outside forces, which have as an end the making of profit. In a very real sense one could say that the system is deplorable, from the point of view of John's interests, because it has treated him simply as a means to an end, paying little regard to his status as an, at least potentially, autonomous person. If this is true of John, it is also true of many 'middle class' people, for example ulcerated executives of advertising companies, bored with their work, yet trapped by the need to service large mortgages, cars and expensive lifestyles.

It may be in the best interests of those hooked on heroin to continue with their habit. It may be in the best interests of those who are hooked on consumerism to continue in their pursuits. Does this leave any room for a programme of legitimate radical social change? Does it not amount to acceptance of the liberal horn of the dilemma posed by the 'paradox of emancipation'? Not entirely – for the implications of taking seriously the central liberal value of autonomy are, as I have stressed, radical.

According to the values which provide the moral foundation of liberal democracy as I have characterised it, a prime aim of social organisation should be to promote as well as possible the autonomy of the people within the society. Being in control of one's own life is, for instance, more important than living a completely pain-free existence. From this standpoint, forms of social organisation which undermine autonomy, are, *ipso facto* to be condemned.

There are two sorts of interest in autonomy – interests in its development and maintenance, and in its exercise. A person's autonomy interests may be harmed either by limiting her capacity for autonomy, or by preventing its exercise.

The main failure of contemporary liberal democratic societies, from the standpoint of one who takes autonomy seriously, is that they seem incompatible with the development and maintenance of the capacity for autonomy in the majority of the population. The allegation would have to be that these societies produce people whose mental state interests are in direct conflict with their autonomy interests. The school system precludes the possibility of any but a minority developing habits of enquiry and critical thinking. The ability to challenge simple arguments from authority is not encouraged. School fits most people for at best, work in hierarchically organised industries, where they are neither required nor able, to take on responsibilities which use creative intelligence. People are subjected to bombardments of advertising, which not only suggest the products advertised are desirable, but also sell ways of life, which are put across as 'normal'. Because of people's fears of being 'abnormal' this pressure constitutes, in effect, a threat. 'If you don't conform to these standards you will be an outsider.'

What about interests in the *exercise* of autonomy? There are different ways in which such interests can be thwarted. The most obvious is by putting control of a person's day-to-day life in the hands of a third party, such as the Court of Protection, which in England handles the affairs of thousands of mentally handicapped people. Another way is by placing restrictions on the choices that are permissible under law. It is illegal to be in possession of heroin, for example. This violates people's interests in the exercise of their autonomy with respect to risk-taking. Another way of restricting the exercise of autonomy is outlawing certain religious or political ideas. In all of these cases control over their own lives is removed to a greater or lesser extent, from people. In many cases it is justifiable, to protect their own interests, either in the future exercise of autonomy, or in the development and maintenance of the capacity, or to protect other vital interests, or to protect the interests of others. One of the main defences of liberal democracy is that at least it offers the best safeguard for people's interests in the exercise of autonomy.

Crude restrictions on freedom to express political opinions constitute a serious violation of citizens' interests in the exercise of autonomy, and they are not to be deplored. However, the response to this should not be to condemn all radical social change. The attempts to maintain allegiance to a political programme by such coercive means are not only morally questionable, but have been shown on many occasions to be *politically* disastrous. It is extremely unlikely that socialism could ever be achieved by such a means.

On the other hand, it is not clear that liberal democracy as presently constituted does offer the best protection even for interests in the *exercise* of such autonomy as people have managed to develop. The poverty of the unemployed and the low paid greatly restrict the choices which are available to them. Workers have effective control neither over their own time, nor over what they produce and how they produce it.

Liberal and radical can unite in seeking to increase the possibilities for the development and exercise of autonomy for people. Their main disagreement is over the best means for achieving these ends. A key task of the radical socialist is to show that the worthy ends of liberalism are irreconcilable not only with Soviet authoritarian 'Communism', but equally with even the more benign forms of capitalism.

In a world of scarce resources it is inevitable that people's interests will sometimes conflict, although in a class-divided society these conflicts may be expected to be especially pervasive. This is no less true for autonomy interests than for those in pleasant mental states. Therefore the principle of respect for autonomy is impracticable in its absolutist form, according to which any infringement on (anyone's) autonomy is morally wrong. However, as Keith Graham (1982) puts it, an advocate of autonomy has:

'A strong motive for stressing the importance of discussion and debate, of canvassing and considering other views before making any final decision about what ought to happen and of exploring the possibilities for compromise. But such attempts to avoid conflict . . . may not always be successful. The question is, what do we do when they are not?' (p.132)

He claims that the person who regards the principle of autonomy as supremely important is committed to being bound by the majority verdict, no matter how perverse their judgment might seem. He defends this by appeal to a principle of maximisation of autonomy. If autonomy is so important, try to minimise its violation, maximise its development and exercise. Although I agree that thwarting the wants of a majority in itself violates more people's interests in the exercise of autonomy, than imposing the wants of the majority on the minority, I cannot accept that in principle this *requires* minority acceptance of the wishes of a majority at a particular time. This is because people exist through time, and there may be an intertemporal conflict of autonomy interests for an individual. Furthermore, the effects of decisions may restrict the autonomy interests of people not enfranchised. *Their* autonomy interests should be represented no less than those within the franchise (for Graham's response to this claim, see Graham, 1982, p.133n; see also Graham, 1986). Certainly at the level of ideal act theory the principle of respect for autonomy should be applied neutrally across time and between people.

Conclusion

If the liberal principle of respect for autonomy is interpreted in the neutralist way suggested here, it is consistent with the principle to restrict someone's autonomy for the sake of autonomy. The clearest case where such a restriction would be justified is within the life of a non-autonomous person, who would otherwise act on false beliefs in an autonomy-reducing manner (young children and the severely mentally disturbed are cases in point). These are the most obvious examples of people suffering from false consciousness about their interests. It is also, in principle, justifiable to restrict the autonomy of one group of people if this is necessary to prevent other people suffering an even worse diminution of autonomy.

Benton characterises the liberal principle as requiring that no policy be implemented without the consent of those who are affected by it. If, among a given population, there is disagreement over an issue, then, other things being equal, respect for autonomy would require that the majority's decision was put into effect, even if this fails to gain the consent of the minority. Future people cannot give their consent to policies at the time they are voted upon. However, any principle of respect for people should give no less weight to future people's interests (subject to discounts for uncertainty). To fail to do this would be to subject these people to arbitrary discrimination. Suppose the policies of a given majority at a particular time will work against the autonomy of future generations. There must be a point beyond which implementing the policies of the majority would pose a more serious violation of people's autonomy than resisting those policies. If this point had been crossed there would be no basic principled objection from concern for autonomy to going against the decision of the present majority.

Having said this, it must be stressed once again that there may be a huge gap between ideal moral theories and their practical counterparts. In practice it is very hard to predict the consequences of particular policies, and previous attempts to impose liberal or egalitarian-sounding values on an unwilling populace have usually ended in disaster, not least for the substantive goals of the values.

Whether or not at the level of political practice this should lead to a decision always to be bound by the desires of a present majority, is an immensely complex issue, which I shall not try to resolve here. My aim has been to shift the terms of the debate over the paradox of emancipation away from conflicts between Stalinism and liberalism, and to relocate it within the heart of liberal principles themselves.

11　Concluding Remarks

Our political leaders have made it known that they would be prepared to fight a nuclear war to defend the freedom of the western world. I do not here wish to discuss whether *anything* is so valuable as to be worth defending by nuclear war. However, one thing is clear: if it is possible even to contemplate that the protection of our freedom may justify nuclear war, then this freedom must be supremely valuable.

Liberal democratic societies pride themselves on their respect for negative liberties such as freedom of expression, freedom of the press and freedom of political association. Whilst I believe these freedoms are very important, they are not intrinsic values. Their main worth consists in being necessary conditions for the development, maintenance and exercise of autonomy. The Kantian view, central to liberal democracy, that it is wrong to treat any individual simply as a means to an end, derives its appeal from the fact that people have the capacity for autonomy. Mill defended the Liberty Principle because he believed that autonomy is constitutive of happiness itself.

In Part II I considered, at a fairly abstract level, different ways of taking autonomy seriously. One conclusion of this part was that there is room for non-neutralist practical principles for promoting autonomy, which are ultimately grounded in a recognition of the desirability of autonomy, neutrally regarded. Discussion of the Liberty Principle revealed that there are very severe difficulties in evaluating general practical principles by reference to the standard of neutral autonomy promotion. It is notoriously difficult to predict the consequences of political programmes; they tend to have all sorts of unintended, and often undesired results.

If autonomy is a vital interest, and if the vital interests of each person are to count equally (as the Kantian principle of respect

186

for people requires), then equal weight should be given to the promotion of all citizens' autonomy. The discussion of children and the mentally disordered strongly suggests that the majority of members of these two groups do particularly badly as far as their autonomy is concerned – in spite of their being naturally disadvantaged. This suggests that liberal democratic societies are failing by the standards of their own value system.

In Chapter 10 I discussed the so-called paradox of emancipation. If it is true that children's autonomy is actually subverted, this has consequences for adults. Without an autonomy-promoting childhood, people are unlikely to become autonomous adults. Heteronomous citizens are likely to be conformist, even if this prevents their own development, and works against the interests of others. Although I prescribe extreme caution, I located the justified opposition to resisting the will of the majority, not in a fundamental principle of respect for autonomy, but at the level of practical principles. Practical principles are historically variable, and there could, theoretically, be a time in which it would actually be justifiable to oppose the will of a given majority, in the name of autonomy.

As I said in the Introduction, the argument about values in this book is hypothetical in form. It is addressed to those who believe that autonomy is a vital interest of human beings, and that human beings should be treated with equal respect, and the conclusion is that there are direct reasons for promoting the most widespread development, maintenance and exercise of autonomy. I have claimed that liberal democratic society has failed to realise this goal. What follows from this?

This claim should be unsettling for a genuine apologist for liberal democratic society. In response to the charge that our society fails adequately to promote its own distinctive fundamental value – in this case autonomy – there are three plausible defences.

The criticisms of liberal democratic society offered here have been to the effect that it falls far short of promoting the most widespread autonomy amongst people. Of course it does not follow from this that there is an *available* system which would do better. To argue seriously about whether socialism indeed does offer a better practical way for promoting autonomy than liberal welfare capitalism would take us far beyond the scope of this book. The liberal's first strategy could be to defend liberal democratic society by claiming that no other promotes autonomy better – 'the Churchillian strategy'. However, the realisation that autonomy is not widely promoted in our society should prompt anyone who values autonomy seriously to study alternative social and political systems to our own.

The second would be to accept that there should be a transformation of the social, political and economic organisation of society. If a class-divided society, with vast inequalities in wealth and power between citizens is inimical to the optimal development of autonomy, then there is a *prima facie* case for seeking a classless, socialist society. Indeed classical Marxism (as distinct from its Leninist perverted forms) places great value on autonomy (even within the liberal interpretation of autonomy offered here). This would retain the fundamental values of liberal democracy, whilst divorcing them from their association with capitalism.

The final strategy would be to question the value of autonomy itself. Many liberals are strongly anti-socialist. Suppose it turned out that autonomy could be best promoted under socialism. Such a liberal would face a dilemma. One way out would be to abandon the belief that autonomy is a fundamental vital interest. This would be a desperate strategy for a liberal, because it amounts to a rejection of liberalism.

Because liberal democratic principles include both a belief in equal respect for the autonomy of all, and a belief that this is consistent with widespread material inequalities, liberal democracy will always be threatened from two sides. On the one hand are those who believe that autonomy can be successfully promoted only by radical socialist transformation. On the other, are the beneficiaries and defenders of the material inequalities, who will tend to suppress autonomy, and move to overt authoritarianism when they see autonomy posing a threat to their privileged position.

Given these tensions it is, perhaps, a minor miracle that liberal democracy has been so stable. Its major critics have historically been socialists, optimistic about the possibility of a better route to promoting liberal values. We are now entering an era where the main threat is coming from an anti-democratic authoritarianism of both the 'left' and the 'right'. The attack from the left comes from those who deny the value of freedom of expression. In seeking to gag their political opponents they seriously threaten the climate of tolerance in which socialist ideas can be given expression. From the 'right', there have been attacks on education, and upon the freedom of radio, television, and local governments to give expression to dissent.

In these times it is especially important to realise that although the civil and political rights protected in liberal democratic society are not *sufficient* for the promotion of autonomy, they are certainly *necessary*. So traditional supporters of liberal democracy should join with socialist critics in defending these rights from their common enemies, whether of the so-called left or right.

Guide to Further Reading

The only other book I am aware of which covers similar ground to that covered in this volume is Young (1986). On the other hand, there is a vast literature on the topics discussed in the different Parts. Consequently, I have divided this guide into three sections, corresponding to the three Parts of the book.

I

For a general discussion of the analysis of concepts in political theory, Rawls (1971) Chapter 1 and Connolly (1983) Chapter 1 are especially useful. The best place to find Kant's theory of rationality and autonomy is Kant (1785). Wolff (1973) offers a comprehensive critical account of *The Groundwork*, and Bennett (1974) Chapter 10 is a penetrating account of Kant's theory of freedom. Hume's views on the role of rationality in action are found in Hume (1739), Book II, Part III, Section III, and Book III, Part I. Also of interest is Hume (1751), Appendix 1. Nagel (1970) offers a stern challenge to a Humean view of rationality, from a Kantian perspective, whereas Parfit (1984), Sections 45 and 46, argues that Hume was mistaken in rejecting the possibility of intrinsically irrational desires. Stroud (1977) gives an accessible, detailed discussion of Hume. The most important passages in Mill for an understanding of autonomy and its significance, are (1859) Chapter III, and (1861) Chapter II. Useful commentaries are Gray (1983), especially Chapter 4, and Ten (1980), especially Chapter 5. Recent discussions of rationality and autonomy which have influenced my own views set out in Chapter 5, include Benn (1976), Davidson (1969), and Frankfurt (1971).

II

Much has been written in the last ten years on ways of interpreting moral principles. Among the most important are Parfit (1984) Chapter 4, Scheffler (1982), especially Chapter 3, and Williams (1976). Mill (1859) Chapters 1 and 5 sets out the classical liberal case for limits on state paternalism. Within the vast contemporary literature on autonomy and the limits of state authority, the following are particularly helpful: Brock (1983), Feinberg (1971) Chapter 2, and Gray (1983) Part III.

III

Harris (1982) offers a radical philosophical argument in favour of granting children extensive political rights. Adams *et. al.* (1972) is a series of essays which shows how children's autonomy is restricted by modern society. Particularly relevant are the essays by Berg, Duane and Neill. A less radical view is defended in Wringe (1984). Freeman (1983) is a comprehensive, well-balanced study of children's rights, from a legal perspective. Chapters 1, 2 and 7 are especially relevant to this book.

The best historical account of the growth of large mental institutions is Scull (1979). Clare (1976) Chapter 2 gives a useful account of different models of mental illness, and Chapter 9 describes the psychiatric services available in Britain. Wing (1978) offers an articulate defence of psychiatry from within the profession – especially relevant are Chapters 2 and 7. Szasz (1961) rejects the whole idea of mental illness, and is very critical of institutionalised psychiatry. Sedgwick (1982) Part 1 offers a searching criticism of the anti-psychiatrists from a socialist perspective, whereas Part 2 gives a critical account of mental health movements, including recent developments in 'community mental health'.

Lewy (1982) is a clear account of false consciousness, which is very critical of the use of the concept by left-wing politicians. Marx (1845–6) provides a clear statement of the control of ideas and attitudes in a class-divided society. The modern classic defence of the view that false consciousness is very pervasive in modern society is Marcuse (1964). Lukes (1974) includes a thought-provoking discussion of problems associated with the view that people may have real interests of which they are completely unaware. Graham (1986) provides a discussion of the difficulties of reconciling democracy, socialism and respect for autonomy.

Bibliography

Adams, P., *et. al.* (1972) *Children's Rights: towards the liberation of the child* (London: Panther Books).

Benn, S. I. (1976) 'Freedom, Autonomy and the Concept of a Person', in *Proceedings of the Aristotelian Society*, vol. 76.

Bennett, J. (1974) *Kant's Dialectic* (Cambridge: Cambridge University Press).

Bennett, J. (1981) 'Morality and Consequences', in McMurrin, S. (ed.), *The Tanner Lectures on Human Values*.

Benton, T. (1982) 'Realism, Power and Objective Interests', in Graham, K. (ed.), (1982).

Berlin, I. (1958) 'Two Concepts of Liberty', reprinted in Berlin, I. (1969), *Four Essays on Liberty* (Oxford: Oxford University Press).

Bloch, S. (1981) 'The Political Misuse of Psychiatry in the Soviet Union', in Bloch, S., and Chodoff, P., (eds), *Psychiatric Ethics* (Oxford: Oxford University Press).

Borger, R., and Cioffi, F. (eds), (1970 *Explanation in the Behavioural Sciences* (Cambridge: Cambridge University Press).

Bottomore, T. B. and Rubel, M. (eds) (1956) *Karl Marx: Selected Writings in Sociology and Social Philosophy* (London: C. A. Watts).

Brandt, R. B. (1979) *A Theory of the Good and the Right* (Oxford: Oxford University Press).

Bristow, R. (1979) 'Why I Decided Not to Become a Teacher', in Hoyles, M. (ed.), *Changing Childhood* (London: Writers and Readers Publishing Co-operative).

Brock, D. (1983) 'Paternalism and Promoting the Good', in Sartorius, R. (ed.), *Paternalism* (Minneapolis: University of Minnesota Press).

Brown, G., and Harris, T. (1978) *Social Origins of Depression* (London: Tavistock).

Cade, B. (1979) 'The Use of Paradox in Therapy', in Walrond-Skinner, S. (ed.), *Family and Marital Psychotherapy: A Critical Approach* (London: Routledge & Kegan Paul).

Clare, A. (1976) *Psychiatry in Dissent* (London: Tavistock).

Connolly, W. (1972 'On "Interests" in Politics', in *Politics and Society*, vol. 2.

Connolly, W. (1983) *The Terms of Political Discourse*, second edition (Oxford: Martin Robertson).

Davidson, D. (1969) 'How is Weakness of Will Possible?' in Feinberg, J. (ed.), *Moral Concepts* (Oxford: Oxford University Press).

Davidson, H. (1967) 'The Double Life of American Psychiatry', in Freeman, H., and Farndale, J. (eds), (1967) *New Aspects of the Mental Health Services* (London: Pergamon Press).

Duane, M. (1972) 'Freedom and the State System of Education', in Adams, P., *et al.*, (1972).

Dubos, R. (1965) *Man Adapting* (New Haven: Yale University Press).

Dworkin, R. (1978) *Taking Rights Seriously* (London: Duckworth).

Elster, J. (1983) *Sour Grapes: Studies in the Subversion of Rationality* (Cambridge: Cambridge University Press).

Feinberg, J. (1971) *Social Philosophy* (Engelwood Cliffs: Prentice Hall).

Frankfurt, H. (1971) 'Freedom of the Will and the Concept of a Person', *Journal of Philosophy* vol. 68.

Freeman, M. D. A. (1983) *The Rights and Wrongs of Children* (London: Pinter).

Freidson, E. (1970) *Professional Dominance* (New York: Atherton).

Glover, J. (1977) *Causing Death and Saving Lives* (Harmondsworth: Penguin).

Glover, J. (1984) *What Sort of People Should There Be?* (Harmondsworth: Penguin).

Goffman, E. (1961) *Asylums* (Garden City, New York: Anchor Books).

Graham, K. (1982) 'Democracy and the Autonomous Moral Agent', in Graham, K. (ed.), (1982), *Contemporary Political Philosophy: Radical Studies* (Cambridge: Cambridge University Press).

Graham, K. (1986) *The Battle of Democracy* (Hassocks: The Harvester Press).

Gray, J. (1983) *Mill On Liberty: A Defence* (London: Routledge & Kegan Paul).

Haksar, V. (1979) *Liberty, Equality and Perfectionism* (Oxford: Oxford University Press).

Hansen, S. and Jensen, J. (1971) *The Little Red School Book*, translated by Berit Thornberry (London: Stage 1).

Hare, R. M. (1981) *Moral Thinking: Its Levels, Method and Point* (Oxford: Oxford University Press).

Harris, J. (1982) 'The Political Status of Children', in Graham, K. (ed.), (1982).

Hobbes, T. (1651) *Leviathan*.

Hollingshead, A. B. and Redlich, F. C. (1958) *Social Class and Mental Illness* (New York).

Honderich, T. (1973) 'One Determinism', in Honderich, T. (ed.), (1973), *Freedom of the Will* (London: Routledge & Kegan Paul).

Hume, D. (1739) *A Treatise of Human Nature*, in Hume (1968).

Hume, D. (1748) *Enquiry into the Human Understanding*, in Hume (1972).

Hume, D. (1751) *Enquiry Concerning the Principles of Morals*, in Hume (1972).

Hume, D. (1968) *A Treatise of Human Nature*, [Reprinted from the Original Edition in three volumes and edited with an analytical index by L. A. Selby-Bigge] (Oxford: Oxford University Press).

Hume, D. (1972) *Enquiries Concerning the Human Understanding and Concerning the Principles of Morals* [Reprinted from the 1777 edition and edited by L. A. Selby-Bigge] (Oxford: Oxford University Press).

Huxley, A. (1955) *Brave New World* (Harmondsworth: Penguin).

Kant, I. (1785) *Groundwork to the Metaphysic of Morals*, in Paton (1948).

Kant, I. (1793) *Religion Within the Limits of Reason Alone*.

Kesey, K. (1973) *One Flew Over the Cuckoo's Nest* (London: Pan Books).

Lewy, G. (1982) *False Consciousness* (New Brunswick: Transaction Books).

Lukes, S. (1974) *Power: A Radical View* (London: Macmillan).

Macpherson, C. B. (1962) *The Political Theory of Possessive Individualism* (Oxford: Oxford University Press).

Macpherson, C. B. (1977) *The Life And Times of Liberal Democracy* (Oxford: Oxford University Press).

Marcuse, H. (1964) *One Dimensional Man* (London: Routledge & Kegan Paul).

Marx, K. (1845–6) *The German Ideology* [The quotation used here was taken from Bottomore, T. B. and Rubel, M. (eds), (1956)].

Maslow, A. (1970) *Motivation and Personality* (New York: Harper & Row).

Mill, J. S. (1859) *On Liberty*. All quotations from John Stuart Mill are taken from *Utilitarianism, On Liberty, and Considerations on Representative Government* (1972) (London: J. M. Dent).

Mill, J. S. (1861) *Utilitarianism*.

Mill, J. S. (1861a) *Considerations on Representative Government*.

Nagel, T. (1970) *The Possibility of Altruism* (Oxford: Oxford University Press).

Neill, A. S. (1972) 'Freedom Works', in Adams, *et al.* (1972).

Nozick, R. (1974) *Anarchy, State and Utopia* (Oxford: Blackwell).

Parfit, D. (1973) 'Later Selves and Moral Principles', in Montefiore, A. (ed.), (1973), *Philosophy and Personal Relations* (London: Routledge & Kegan Paul).

Parfit, D. (1984) *Reasons and Persons* (Oxford: Oxford University Press).

Paton, H. J. (ed.), (1948), *The Moral Law*, (London: Hutchinson [edition of Immanuel Kant's *Groundwork of the Metaphysic of Morals*].

Rawls, J. (1971) *A Theory of Justice* (Oxford: Oxford University Press).

Redlich, F. C. and Kellert, S. R. (1978) 'Trends in American Mental Health', in *American Journal of Psychiatry*, vol. 135.

Scheffler, S. (1982) *The Rejection of Consequentialism* (Oxford: Oxford University Press).

Smart, J. and Williams, B. (1973) *Utilitarianism: For and Against* (Cambridge: Cambridge University Press).

Scull, A. (1977) *Decarceration: Community Treatment and the Deviant – A Radical View* (Englewood Cliffs: Prentice-Hall).

Scull, A. (1979) *Museums of Madness* (London: Allen Lane).

Sedgwick, P. (1982) *Pscyho Politics* (London: Pluto).

Spitzko, E. C. (1883) *Insanity: Its Classification, Diagnosis and Treatment* (New York: Bermeigham & Co.).

Stevens, O. (1982) *Children Talking Politics: Political Learning in Childhood* (Oxford: Martin Robertson).

Stroud, B. (1977) *Hume* (London: Routledge & Kegan Paul).

Szasz, T. (1961) *The Myth of Mental Illness* (New York: Hoeber Harper).

Szasz, T. (1971) *The Manufacture of Madness* (London: Routledge & Kegan Paul). [Quote from 1973 edition, London: Paladin.]

Ten, C. L. (1980) *Mill on Liberty* (Oxford: Oxford University Press).

Walvin, J. (1982) *A Child's World* (Harmondsworth: Penguin).

Whitehead, T. (1982) *Mental Illness and the Law* (Oxford: Blackwell).

Wikler, D. (1979) 'Paternalism and the Mildly Retarded', in *Philosophy and Public Affairs*, vol. 8.

Williams, B. (1965) 'Ethical Consistency', reprinted in Williams (1973).

Williams, B. (1970) 'Deciding to Believe', reprinted in Williams (1973).

Williams, B. (1973) *Problems of the Self* (Cambridge: Cambridge University Press).

Williams, B. (1973a) 'A Critique of Utilitarianism', in Smart, J. and Williams, B. (1973).

Williams, B. (1976) 'Persons, Character and Morality', reprinted in Williams (1981).

Williams, B. (1981) *Moral Luck* (Cambridge: Cambridge University Press).

Williams, H. (1983) *Kant's Political Philosophy* (Oxford: Blackwell).

Wing, J. K. (1978) *Reasoning About Madness* (Oxford: Oxford University Press).

Wolff, R. P. (1973) *The Autonomy Of Reason* (New York: Harper & Row).

Wringe, C. (1984) *Democracy, Schooling and Political Education* (London: George Allen & Unwin).

Young, R. (1986) *Personal Autonomy: Beyond Negative and Positive Liberty* (London: Croom Helm).

Index

abortion 121
absolute pacificism 79f, 97f
acts/omissions doctrine 81f
Adams, P. 191
Aegeus and Theseus 95f, 102, 110
agent-relativism 84–93
  prerogatives and requirements 87f
anti-sychiatry 145–9
Aristotle 104
autonomy
  a matter of degree 51, 106f
  and agent relativism 91ff
  and authorship 20, 21f
  and liberal democracy 3, 7–10, 61f, 70, 71, 113, 115, 118, 120, 132f, 139, 144, 163f, 165f, 177f, 181–5, 186–9
  and moral responsibility 16, 22–6, 46, 53
  and neutrality 82–93
  and positive liberty 6
  and treating people as ends in themselves 13f, 20f, 75–82, 95, 107, 110f, 120, 121f, 123, 142, 150, 181, 186
  as a goal 74–82, 134, 150, 183f
  as a vital interest 45, 52–61, 106–9, 115, 120, 170
  capacity for and exercise of 69, 88
  heteronomy versus non-autonomy 14ff
  regional versus individual 5f
  requiring rationality 26

Baker, J. M. x, 107, 143
Begin, M. 1
Benn, S. 190
Bennett, J. 23, 82, 190
Bentham, J. 45, 59, 74, 83, 93, 104
Benton, T. 169, 176, 184
Berg, L. 191
Berlin, I. 6, 8
Bloch, S. 151
Borger, R. 68
Brandt, R. 34
Brave New World 44ff, 47, 74, 155
Bristow, R. 135
Brock, D. 191
Brown, G. 155, 162
Bruce, E. x
Buridan's Ass 41

Cade, B. 86
Camp David Agreement 2, 3, 5
Carter, J. 1
Churchill, W. 168
Cioffi, F. 68
Clare, A. 161, 191
community mental health care 152ff
conceptions, adequacy of 3f
Connolly, W. 175f, 190
Court of Protection 182

Davidson, D. 190
Davidson, H. 159
Declaration of Hawaii 140
deliberation, ideal 33–9
Descartes, R. 48

DesJardins, G. x
double effect 82
Duane, M. 138, 191
Dubos, R. 148
Dworkin, R. 177

Education Act (1870) 119
Elster, J. 86f
Engels, F. 166, 167

Feinberg, J. 191
Fellows, R. x
Frankfurt, H. 64–7, 122f, 190
Freeman, M.D.A. 191
Freidson, E. 149

Glover, J. x, 82
Goffman, E. 151
Graham, K. x, 183f, 191
Gray, J. 55, 104, 190, 191

Haksar, V. 177
Hall, R. x
happiness 120
eudaimonia 104
the general happiness 103,
105, 112
Hare, R. M. 80f
Harris, J. x, 118, 191
Harris, T. 155, 162
higher and lower pleasures 55–61
Hitler, A. 17
Hobbes, T. 100ff
Holmes, J. x
Honderich, T. 25
Hopkins, J. x
Hospital Plan (1962) 152
Hollingshead, A. B. 159
Huberty, J. 79f, 98
human nature, transformation
of 101f
Hume, D. 11, 27, 28–43, 44, 55,
56, 61, 63, 64, 70, 190
Huxley, A. 44f, 74, 155

imperatives, categorical versus
hypothetical 19

interests
and hypothetical choices 33–9,
56–61, 175ff, 178
vital 58–61, 106f

Jones, P. x

Kant, I. 11–27, 28–33, 42, 43, 44,
52f, 55, 59, 61, 63, 70, 74–82,
89, 107, 121f, 123, 132, 142,
144, 150, 186
Kaye, Danny 1
Kellert, S. R. 159
Kesey, K. 145

Lenin, V. I. 168, 188
Lewy, G. 166, 191
liberty, negative and positive 6, 8
Lukes, S. 165, 175f

Macdonald, G. x
Macpherson, C. B. 8, 101, 165
Marcuse, H. 173f, 178, 191
Marx, K. 101, 167, 172, 188, 191
Maslow, A. 53
Mehring, F. 166
Mental Health Act (1959) 145,
151
Mill, J. S. 11, 27, 44–62, 63, 70,
74, 93, 102–113, 117, 123f,
128ff, 133, 134, 170, 172, 174,
176f, 186, 190
moral constraints and goals 73f,
134
and moral conflicts 74–82
moral theory, complexity of 97ff
Murdoch, I. 68

Nagel, T. 38, 89, 92, 190
needs
and human nature 53–61
false 173–9
Neill, A. S. 137, 191
Nozick, R. 58, 74

O'Hear, A. x
Othello 49

Parfit, D.   x, 34, 40, 87, 92, 97, 190
paternalism   95f, 115f, 171f, 184
   and children   111, 117ff, 123f, 134
   and the mildly retarded   141–4
   state   102–112, 177, 182
   strong and weak   110f
Pettit, P.   x
Plato   68, 167
psychotherapy   155, 159f
psychotropic drugs   155f

racism   124f
rationality
   and ends   17, 29ff, 42f, 47, 67, 70
   and neutrality   17–19, 37ff
   civil service model of   30f
   essentially irrational
      desires   39ff
   irrationality versus non-
      rationality   14ff, 121f
   theoretical rationality and
      truth   33f, 46–52
Rawls, J.   3, 89, 115, 117, 177, 190
Redlich, F. C.   159

Sadat, A.   1
Sayers, M.   x
Sayers, P.   x
Scheffler, S.   84, 88, 190
Scull, A.   152, 158, 161, 191
Sedgwick, P.   147ff, 154, 156, 158, 191
self-defeating views, directly and
   indirectly self-defeating   87–93, 98
Socrates   56

Sorell, T.   x
Spitzka, E. C.   147
Stalin, J.   168, 169
Stern, W.   141
Stevens, O.   127
Stroud, B.   29, 190
suffragette movement   128
Swift, Jonathan   14
Szasz, T.   145ff, 191

Teamsters Union   125

utilitarianism
   and neutralist
      consequentialism   83f, 104
   Benthamite and Millian
      versions   45, 59, 104–9, 134
   'milk bottle' version   83

values, instrumental and
   intrinsic   73f

Walvin, J.   119
war of all against all   100ff
Weale, A.   x
Whitehead, T.   140f, 151
Wikler, D.   141–4
will
   as faculty of choice   14–17, 121
   freedom of   32f, 64–8, 122
   heteronomy of   63–8
Williams, B.   47, 80, 85–93, 190
Williams, H.   74
Wing, J. K.   148, 152, 153, 158, 159, 191
Wolff, R. P.   23, 190
Wringe, C.   191

Young, R.   190